COMMANDO

COMMANDO

Memoirs of a Fighting Commando in World War Two

Brigadier John Durnford-Slater
DSO and Bar

Naval Institute Press
Annapolis, Maryland

Published and distributed in the United States of America
by the Naval Institute Press, Annapolis, Maryland 21402.

Library of Congress Catalog Card No. 91-60981

ISBN 1-55750-125-4

Publishing History
Commando was first published in 1953
(William Kimber and Co. Limited)
and is reproduced now exactly as the original edition,
complete and unabridged.

Quality printing and binding by
Biddles Limited, Woodbridge Park,
Guildford, Surrey, GU1 1DA, England

PREFACE

THE officers and men of No. 3 Commando, like all the army Commandos, were volunteers who were prepared to take their chance. Some got away with it and some did not. They all took plenty of chances.

What were the driving motives behind it all? In the beginning there was the fascination of the unknown. They were taking on a new phase of warfare against the unbeaten German army. The excitement of it all appealed to everybody. There was the happiness of working in good company, with picked volunteers in a star unit. Later, pride in the unit and in the traditions of early operations took the place of novelty and excitement. By 1943 all had had their fill of excitement. They were always chosen for the most hazardous operations, and they appreciated the compliment.

Above all there was the satisfaction of doing a good job for a great King, who had visited and encouraged us in our early days.

In their five years of operations, No. 3 Commando had their full share of triumph and disaster. Directly one operation was finished, planning started for the next one. Casualties were many, and this never ceased to horrify me.

The Commando tradition of always maintaining the impetus of the advance lasted to the end.

Bedford,
January, 1953
John Durnford-Slater

OPERATIONS
by
Nº3 COMMANDO.
1940-45.

VAAGSO

Scapa Flow

Larus

GUERNSEY

DIEPPE
'D' DAY

Gibraltar

FOTEN IS

Berlin

R. RHINE
OSNABRUCK
R. WESER
R. ALLER
R. ELBE

ITALY

SICILY

Port Said.

W.R.DALZELL

ACKNOWLEDGEMENT

I WOULD like to thank Brigadier Peter Young, D.S.O., M.C., for his kindness in allowing me to make use of his diaries for reference and to quote a substantial passage from them in connection with the D-Day landings.

J.D.-S.

CONTENTS

ILLUSTRATIONS
Appearing between pages 94 and 95

ILLUSTRATIONS

No. 3 Commando Bridge

General Montgomery visiting us at Termoli

The Author leaving Buckingham Palace with his wife and daughter after being awarded the D.S.O

Watching for snipers in Osnabruck

Wesel: on guard against German rearguards

"The party took place three hundred yards from the front line."

Brigadier B. W. Leicester, the Author, and Brigadier D. Mills-Roberts

Meeting No. 3 Commando at Tilbury, 1945

No. 3 Commando leaving Tilbury

Disbandment, Victoria Station

Afterwards: Charlie Head, the Author, and John Charles Head

Most of the illustrations are reproduced by permission of the Imperial War Museum

MAPS

Chapter I

"THE HUNTER CLASS"

WHEN the letter came, in mid-June, 1940, Dunkirk was past and the last of the B.E.F. had been evacuated from France. The letter called for volunteers to raid the enemy coast. I liked that. "Men of good physique," "able to swim and navigate boats," "initiative and leadership," "hazardous work." Those were the phrases in it.

I was tired of training men for action: I wanted action myself.

I tore upstairs and burst in to see my Commanding Officer, Colonel J. V. Naisby, a tall, competent artillery officer of about forty. I waved the letter before him.

"Here's exactly the thing I want to do," I said. "Will you release me?"

I was Adjutant of his unit, the 23rd Medium and Heavy Training Regiment, Royal Artillery. We were stationed at Plymouth.

"Calm yourself, John," the Colonel said, eyeing me with mild disapproval; and he reached for the letter. He read it and put it down with a sigh. "But we've plenty of work here. Who's going to do your job?"

It took fifteen minutes to win him round.

"I can see you've made up your mind," he said, finally.

"Thank you, sir. I'll need a recommendation from you, of course."

He looked up at me, rubbing his chin. Suddenly he grinned.

"You're an old soldier, John: write your own recommendation. I'll sign it." Which we did.

There was a War Office interview, of course. Then I was back in Plymouth, and almost before I had time to settle back into my old routine, Colonel Naisby walked into my room. He seemed pleased.

11

"That must have been a good recommendation I signed," he remarked, and dropped a signal on my desk. It read:

CAPT. J. F. DURNFORD SLATER ADJUTANT 23RD MEDIUM AND HEAVY TRAINING REGT. R.A. IS APPOINTED TO RAISE AND COMMAND NUMBER 3 COMMANDO IN THE RANK OF LIEUT. COLONEL. GIVE EVERY ASSISTANCE AND RELEASE FROM PRESENT APPOINTMENT FORTHWITH AS OPERATIONAL ROLE IMMINENT.

At that time No. 1 Commando and No. 2 Commando did not exist: it had originally been intended to form them as airborne units, a policy which was subsequently abandoned. This made me the first Commando soldier of the war. I had wanted action: I was going to get it. I should have been delighted to join in any rank, but was naturally pleased to get command. I was confident I could do the work and made up my mind to produce a really great unit. I owed it to my mother.

My mother had a strong will. Her father had been in the army, and so had her husband. My father, Captain L. F. Slater, was a regular officer in the Royal Sussex Regiment. I last saw him on the 5th August, 1914, when I was five and a half years old; he had come to join us on holiday at Milton-on-Sea, before leaving for France with the B.E.F. I remember that just before his arrival I had an encounter with a small boy who told me he was German. I promptly struck him on the nose, drawing blood. I was being led away toward the chastisement I deserved when my father arrived and distracted Mother from her purpose. My father was killed in action a month later; and my mother made it clear to me that I should follow him into the army. She put me down for Wellington, the school with the strongest army tradition in Britain.

I entered Wellington when I was thirteen. The thing I hated at once was the Officers' Training Corps. I didn't like the uniform, the marching, the drill, or anything else about it. I dreaded the coming of Wednesday, the Corps day.

"What's the matter with you, Slater, can't you march in step?" the instructor would yell.

He told me my uniform was untidy. He shook his head and muttered at me under his breath. It took me only a few weeks to see that I was not meant for the army. When I mentioned this to my mother, she explained, with a great deal of determination, that I was wrong. Gradually, I learned how to march in step; but I still disliked it.

"The army's the best life for you, John," my mother kept telling me when I went home. "You'll never like it in business."

My home was in the village of Instow, North Devon. There were several people who lived there in retirement after a life in the Argentine. They told me of the limitless pampas, and of the horses. By the time I was fourteen, I told my mother that I was bound and determined to go to the Argentine and breed horses. My mother said that she doubted if I could succeed on the very limited capital which would be at my disposal.

"The army is your best chance," she declared firmly. "If you go into the artillery, you'll have your horses too."

That was the extent of her willingness to compromise: originally she had wanted me to join the Royal Sussex Regiment, like my father.

My mother's character was stronger than mine. I entered Woolwich at eighteen, and a year and a half later my army career had begun in earnest in the Royal Artillery. It was 1929.

I was sent to India for six years. There was first-rate sport: football, cricket, hockey, plenty of riding, and pig-sticking. Regiments were up to strength and the men were first-class and really good company, well-trained and keen. It was a pleasure and privilege to work with them. But when I returned to Britain in 1935, I found everything changed. The army at home was at its lowest ebb. Regiments were under strength and equipment was very short. I missed the company of the fine men we had had in India. Instead of these men we had to deal with raw recruits who were mostly posted to India as soon as they became efficient soldiers. Each day was a frustration. I wanted to resign—until Munich. Then I thought, why bother? War seemed inevitable. Up to then, I felt, I had only been playing at soldiering.

When the war came, I was Adjutant on the only anti-aircraft unit which was operational in south-west England. Soon other regiments arrived and our duties became routine. It seemed time to do something about becoming a fighting soldier. Told I was more valuable training troops in England, I was posted as Adjutant to a newly-formed training regiment. The work *was* valuable, but painfully dull.

Then the War Office letter came, and dullness vanished.

On the 4th June, 1940, immediately following the completion of the Dunkirk evacuation, Mr. Churchill in his speech to the House of Commons declared: "We shall not be content with a defensive war." That same afternoon he wrote to General Ismay, his right-hand man in the War Cabinet Secretariat: "We should immediately set to work to organise self-contained, thoroughly equipped raiding units." Two days later he wrote, "Enterprises must be prepared with specially trained troops of the hunter class who can develop a reign of terror down the enemy coasts. I look to the joint Chiefs of Staff to propose measures for vigorous enterprise and ceaseless offensive against the whole German-occupied coastline, leaving a trail of German corpses behind them."

These promptings by Mr. Churchill brought about the formation of the Commandos. Under pressure from him the various army commands were instructed to call for volunteers for "special service of a hazardous nature." Ten Commandos of five hundred men each were to be formed.

The War Office letter which I had received implemented this decision and called for volunteers for these new Commandos.

The Germans were forming up on the other side of the Channel. It seemed that invasion could not be far off. I saw General Sir Robert Haining, then Deputy Chief of the Imperial General Staff. He impressed upon me the importance of forming No. 3 Commando as quickly as possible, and suggested that I should form it in Plymouth.

"You might have to operate in a fortnight," he said.

I was given Southern Command as my recruiting ground.

Fortunately, I had had pre-war experience in the selection of territorial officers. This helped. From volunteers who, like myself, had answered that first letter, I made my choice. I wanted cheerful officers, not groaners. A good physique was important, but size was not. I looked for intelligence and keenness.

If I found a man I thought would do, I telephoned his former civilian employers in my own time during the evening. I looked for some indication of success, of initiative. If he was a regular officer, I checked up on his record of service and tried to find someone I knew to tell me if he was a suitable type. I was in a mad hurry, but I had to find first-class officers. I visited the headquarters towns of the Southern Command, Weymouth, Salisbury, Winchester, Oxford, Exeter, to interview the candidates.

I travelled and interviewed, interviewed and travelled non-stop: until, finally, I had the officers I needed. Then I sent them out in teams of three to comb the command for other ranks. Each team of three officers was given a selection of units from which to choose men to form their troop. I gave them four days to select their men and to get them to Plymouth.

My appointment had come through on the 28th June. By the 5th July No. 3 Commando was in existence. The Commando consisted of ten troops, each of three officers and forty-seven men; so, with my headquarters, I had a strength of thirty-five officers and five hundred men. Instead of putting troops into barracks the Commando system was to give each man a subsistence allowance of 6s. 8d. a day; the man was then required to find his own accommodation and food. This was in every way a splendid arrangement, it increased a man's self-reliance and self-respect, developed his initiative and made him available for training at any time of the day or night. Nobody had to be left in barracks for administrative duties and every officer and man was able to concentrate entirely on training; the old barrack-room boredom and bad language were eliminated. Furthermore, wherever we went we were always welcomed by our landladies, who took a pride in the unit and did everything to help the men they were billetting. I merely allotted an area of

Plymouth to each troop and left the officers and men to find their own accommodation.

The first selection of officers and men was good. Nobody in a ten-minute interview can be sure, but the proof of the high quality of our initial intake is the high performance which many of our original members gave in the years to come. After a week I found that I had nine good troops and that one troop was indifferent and undisciplined. A fine man named Edgington, now landlord of the White Hart Hotel, Hayle, Cornwall, was Troop Sergeant Major of this bad troop. He gave me great assistance in putting things right. From the start, Commando leaders had the power to return to their units any unsuitable officer or man. This process, known as "R.T.U." was freely applied to my bad troop. Throughout the existence of No. 3 Commando I made very free use of the "R.T.U." punishment, particularly in the case of officers.

The first intake of officers and men contained all sorts of interesting characters. On the whole the type I looked for was the quiet, modest type of Englishman, who knew how to laugh and how to work. Other Commandos were formed especially for the Scots and the Irish, although we had quite a few of these mixed up with our core of Englishmen. I always avoided anyone who talked too much, and soon learned a lesson in this when a fine athletic-looking fellow who had taken part in many sports proved useless and boastful and had to be discharged. We never enlisted anybody who looked like the tough-guy criminal type, as I considered that this sort of man would be a coward in the battle.

Typical of the best type of our initial intake was Private George Herbert of the Northampton Regiment. He joined us, having already won the M.M. at Dunkirk, and was subsequently awarded the D.C.M. In 1943 he was commissioned in the field and proved to be just as good an officer as he had been a private soldier. He had pre-war regular service and was a cobbler by trade. George was the perfect example of soldier, officer and gentleman. He was of medium height, with dark flashing eyes. The first time I met him was a few days after we arrived at Plymouth, when he and another soldier came before me in the office. Lieutenant Peter Young was his Section Commander and produced the charge sheet. The charge was, "conduct to the prejudice of good order and military discipline, i.e. fighting in billets." There had been a dispute over a matter of two pounds and Herbert had stuck a knife into the other fellow. Young brought them in. They were two fine looking men, very smart, and stood strictly to attention. The charge was read out by the Regimental Sergeant Major who also produced the knife and the money. There was no evidence as to whose money it was. Herbert was an M.M. and I didn't want to lose him. If I didn't send Herbert away I couldn't send the other fellow.

"We can't tolerate this sort of behaviour, fighting in civilian billets, particularly with knives. I'll have to send you both back to your units," I told them.

"Give us whatever punishment you think fit, but don't send us back to our units," Herbert said.

I then asked Peter Young for their characters and he spoke well of them both.

I said: "Well, divide the money; the next small charge against either of you and out you go."

It was my impression that Herbert was right but it was merely one man's word against the other. Herbert had a wonderful record at Dunkirk and M.M.s were very rare in those days. He had had a hell of a battle in France and hadn't fully unwound yet. In later days he always maintained that I owed him a pound.

Private Johnny Dowling came to us from the Durham Light Infantry. He was small, only about five feet five, was full of life and a wonderful boxer and soldier. He had learned his boxing at Father Murphy's St. Malachy's Club in Liverpool and subsequently spent three seasons in the boxing booths, where Gus Foran was one of his sparring partners. I first got to know him after seeing him box, and he was equally good company whether in the gymnasium, in battle, or merely talking about some past or projected operation; he was always as much at ease talking to generals as to private soldiers. Action was what he wanted whether in the boxing ring or in the battle.

Corporal Lofty King of the Rifle Brigade was very tall and

very tough. He was a hard fellow in many ways, and very hard with his men; he didn't give a damn if he knocked a man down. Sometimes I told him he was being too rough; Lofty would say:

"It's good for them, Colonel; it won't do them any harm."

He would mean it and believe it. He genuinely enjoyed fighting and looked happiest, and indeed inspired, in battle. In the field he was kinder to his men, as if the fighting were a kind of release for him.

Peter Young joined us as a second lieutenant. He left us in 1945 as a brigadier, with the D.S.O. and three M.C.s. He was of medium height, very intelligent, very cunning and strong, with a caustic tongue. He had done well at Dunkirk and found that he liked action. He didn't fancy staying in England and thought that he would get experience and promotion in the Commandos. Peter was full of ideas and full of work; he kept working out new ideas to improve the troop attack, continuously seeking perfection. He would say:

"I think I've improved this troop attack; will you come tomorrow morning and see me demonstrate it?"

I always went and always found his ideas good.

"The Colonel will take No. 3 in the movement group," he would order.

And I then had to go through whatever arduous exercise his fertile brain had invented. As an artilleryman I thus personally learned the craft of the infantry the hard way. I found that there was plenty to learn.

Lieutenant Algy Forrester did not actually join us for a week, but was on the doorstep within ten minutes of the office opening in Plymouth. He kept worrying the Administrative Officer, "I am not going away until I see the Colonel"; and he continually pestered me until I got him into the unit. Algy, like Lofty King, had the killer instinct in a big way and was quite ruthless in driving people hard and in sacking anyone unsuitable.

Lieutenant Charlie Head from Helston, Cornwall, was also an original starter. In September, 1938, I was posted as Adjutant of a territorial regiment in Cornwall. My Colonel was a very able Cornishman named Barbary. He was justly proud of his Cornish ancestry and of his achievement in making his way in life from being a village carpenter to being one of the head men of Bickford Smith, the fuse specialists of Camborne; he had never troubled to alter his Cornish way of speaking. Shortly after my arrival he took me to Helston where the brothers Charlie and Jack Head were in charge of the local contingent of the territorials. Colonel Barbary introduced me to the Heads using these words:

"Don't 'ee go out with they boy 'Eads 'cept 'ee got a bellyful of food inside 'ee."

Over the years I found this advice to be very sound. When I applied to Colonel Barbary for the release of Charlie Head in order that he might join No. 3 Commando the Colonel wrote a letter to the War Office saying that it was highly undesirable that we should serve together. He thought we were too lighthearted.

An incident in the first fortnight of the war, while we were both serving in Colonel Barbary's Anti-aircraft Regiment at Plymouth, brought matters to a head. One evening Charlie and I had taken two A.T.S. girls out for a couple of beers in Devonport. We had known them both well when they were civilians back in Cornwall. They now worked at the A.T.S. officers' mess, and after we had all sipped beer for an hour or so they said they must get back to serve dinner there. One was cook, the other mess waitress. During dinner the waitress stumbled with a bowl of soup which, unfortunately, flew into the lap of a senior A.T.S. officer.

Under angry cross-examination the girl admitted at last that she had been "out for a beer with John Durnford-Slater and Charlie Head."

"Those two officers are a bad influence on our girls," the high-ranking, soup-stained A.T.S. complained to Colonel Barbary.

He agreed. In fact he decided that we were also a bad influence on one another. Charlie was promptly posted away to Weymouth. In some ways he was absolutely right; in August, 1952, I wrote a list of over fifty incidents in which we had been involved together, each one of which might have led to one or other, or both, of us being court-martialled; all, I am glad to say, good clean fun. I started counting the irregularities we had committed, but discarded this task as hopeless. The Colonel was also, however, absolutely wrong. Like many of our critics, he did not realise that when Charlie Head and I went to war, fooling and liquor were put aside and our joint energies concentrated on the opposition. Sometimes we had to go to war on pompous staff officers on our own side and sometimes on the Germans or Italians.

Charlie Head was another tall man, full of character and laughter. At the age of sixteen he had joined the Merchant Service and served his time. Then at twenty-one he started to train as a veterinary surgeon with the object of joining his father in practice at Helston. He proved a most successful vet; also he had an exact knowledge of human nature and, being a born leader, soon mastered the technique of Commando work. As a raconteur I have never known his equal; I have seen him reduce people of all sorts to helpless laughter with simple stories of our doings. In battle he was always taking the lead and was quite oblivious of danger. Charlie was destined to serve me in all sorts of capacities, including those of Signals Officer and Adjutant.

Private Charlesworth of the Lancashire Fusiliers was a typical regular soldier and product of Lancashire. Always cheerful and always quick-witted, he served me for years as a most faithful batman.

What I was seeking and what I obtained were men of character beyond the normal. I considered that morale was the most important single factor making for success in war; that is the spirit which moves men willingly to strive and to endure. I intended that every soldier in the Commandos should be a potential leader; that he must be mentally and physically tough and must radiate cheerfulness, enthusiasm and confidence. The characters described are typical of our first selection.

I remember our first troop commanders' meeting. It was held upstairs in a small requisitioned house which we had obtained as a headquarters in a Plymouth back street. Plymouth had been selected as our first station on account of the training facilities, both naval and military. I sat behind a bare table. The troop commanders formed a semi-circle around me. They looked good, they were young, keen and fit, and they leaned forward eagerly to listen.

"We're going to operate months before anyone else," I said, "it's up to us to make ourselves the greatest unit of all time."

I meant it. Why not? Every man and officer in the unit had been hand-picked and had the true volunteer spirit.

Chapter II

GUERNSEY

BY mid-July we had launched our first operation across the Channel against the enemy. If the pace was dizzy it seemed exciting at the time. Looking back, I can see that under such rushed conditions, with no experience, no proper landing craft and inadequate training, this first operation was foredoomed to failure. Later, the very word "Commando" was to become synonymous with perfectly trained, tough, hard-fighting, and skilled specialists. You don't achieve that overnight.

I was called to London to help plan this first operation. Captain David Niven, the film star, who was a staff officer in the small Combined Operations Headquarters, helped to brief me. I found him a model of what a staff officer should be, lucid, keen, able and helpful. The operation was to be a small-scale raid on Guernsey, mainly to capture prisoners and inflict casualties. On the 2nd July, 1940, Mr. Churchill wrote to General Ismay:

"If it be true that a few hundred German troops have been landed on Jersey or Guernsey, plans should be studied to land secretly by night and kill or capture the invaders. Exactly an exploit for which the Commandos would be suited."

No doubt General Ismay passed this note on to the small organisation then running Combined Operations, who, not having at that time the necessary troops and landing craft for a major operation, decided on the small reconnaissance which duly took place on the 17th July.

We knew nothing of what had happened on the island since the Germans had landed there. Accordingly, on the 8th July, a native of Guernsey named Lieutenant Nicolle was landed

22

there by submarine. He was picked up three days later with information. The German force, he said, numbered 469; they had machine-gun posts all along the coast; and their main concentration was in St. Peter's Port so that any part of the island could be reinforced within twenty minutes of an alarm.

The plan was that two old destroyers on the night of the 12th–13th July would carry our raiding force to Guernsey. The force was one troop of No. 3 Commando and No. 11 Independent Company. Our troop was to create a diversion for No. 11's attack on the island's airfield. I selected H Troop, as this one was mostly formed of regular soldiers who had operated at Dunkirk and so were likely to be well forward in their training; the troop contained such characters as Peter Young, George Herbert and Charlesworth. I decided to go myself as well, with a small party from our headquarters. The destroyers, H.M.S. *Scimitar* and H.M.S. *Saladin*, were to be accompanied by six R.A.F. air-sea rescue launches which would put us to our landing beaches at 12.50 a.m. The destroyers were to wait for us two hours, not an instant longer.

That was the plan.

At the last moment the date was postponed until the night of the 14th–15th July. Since we were to sail from Dartmouth, I had breakfast at the Royal Castle Hotel on the morning of the 14th. I was excited, naturally, at being on the verge of our first operation, a very secret affair of course, and it came as rather a shock when I saw my sister Helen sitting at the next table with her husband, Admiral Franklin. Helen saw me and smiled happily.

"Hallo, John! What on earth are you doing here?"

"We've got some troops training in the area," I said. "What are *you* doing?"

She said they were down to visit their son at the Royal Naval College. I felt uneasy but tried not to appear so. Fortunately, for the strain was growing, I was called out to the foyer of the hotel a few minutes later. An officer from Combined Operations Staff had just come off the night train from London.

He said: "Colonel, the whole plan has been changed. Jerry

is too strong. He's been reinforced at some of the places where we had intended to land."

We moved into a bedroom of the hotel and worked out a new plan on the spot. Now we were to land in Telegraph Bay on the south side of the island, just west of the Jerbourg Peninsula; and not on the north coast as originally decided. We were to sail at six o'clock that evening. Our role was still to create a diversion for the Independent Company which was to attack the airfield under Colonel Ronnie Tod, who was later to join No. 9 Commando and to become one of the most successful Commando soldiers of the war.

We completed our preparations in the gymnasium of the Royal Naval College, Dartmouth. Many of the weapons had been specially brought from London, as tommy guns and Brens were in very short supply and could only be issued for actual operations. We obtained the help of some cadets from the college who thoroughly enjoyed the work of loading the magazines and helping us in general. We planned the approach with the naval commanders and started to brief the men. Before we realised it, it was a quarter to six, and we had to embark hurriedly in the destroyer. It was a lovely summer evening and as we steamed out of the harbour most of the town was out walking on the quay. I wondered what they thought of our strange-looking convoy.

I went over the final details with my officers in the cabin of the *Scimitar's* Captain on the way across. We had been so busy all day, dealing with naval officers and obtaining and issuing our special weapons, that this was the first chance our officers had had to discuss it all together.

Lieutenant Joe Smales's party was to establish a road block on the road leading from the Jerbourg Peninsula to the rest of the island, so that we should not be interrupted by German reinforcements. My own party were to attack a machine-gun post and to put the cable hut at the foot of the Peninsula out of action. Captain V. T. G. de Crespigny, the Troop Commander of H Troop, with the main party, was to attack the barracks situated on the Peninsula, and Peter Young was to guard the beach. Peter did not relish this job as he wanted more action.

"All right," I told him, "if it's quiet, come forward and see what's going on."

"You chaps satisfied with the arrangements?" I asked finally. They nodded. We synchronised our watches.

The password for the operation was "Desmond."

Somewhere on the way across two of our air-sea rescue launches dropped out with motor trouble. They had been assigned to the Independent Company, not to us. Just after midnight I went out on deck. It was a moonless night, but presently, from a couple of miles off, I could just distinguish the cliffs on the south side of Guernsey, dark, foreboding, and very high. We crept along the length of the island. At about a quarter to one I saw our gap in the cliff, the place where we were to climb to the top. On our right, Telegraph Point reached out into the sea. Our two launches slid alongside the destroyer and we clambered down on rope nettings. The sea was calm. It was dead easy.

The launches purred away from the mother ship. The naval officers in charge of the launches started off on the agreed course, watching their compasses carefully. My own eyes were on the cliffs, and I was astonished to note that we were heading out to sea in the direction of Brittany. "This is no bloody good," I said to the skipper of our launch, "we're going right away from Guernsey."

He looked up from his compass for the first time. Then he looked back and saw the cliff.

"You're right! We are indeed. It must be this damn degaussing arrangement that's knocked the compass out of true. I ought to have had it checked."

"Don't worry about the compass: let's head straight for the beach."

"Right!"

About a hundred yards from the beach a black silhouette seemed to approach from our port side. In undertones some of the men murmured, "U-boat!"

Momentarily my heart sank. What a mug's game this was! Why hadn't I stayed at home, in warmth and comfort? Then I realised that the U-boat was only a rock which bore the exact shape of a submarine superstructure.

At that moment the launches, simultaneously and side by side, hit bottom. As they had not been designed as landing craft, they drew several feet of water. Besides, as the plan had been postponed for forty-eight hours, the tide was not half-way out. It was high. The bottom, instead of smooth sand as had been calculated, was studded with boulders. I jumped in, armpit-deep. A wave hit me on the back of the neck and caused me to trip over a rock. All around me officers and men were scrambling for balance, falling, coming up and coughing salt water.

I doubt if there was a dry weapon amongst us. Once on shore, we loosened the straps of our battledress to let the sea pour out. Then, with a sergeant named Knight close behind me, I set off running up the long flight of concrete steps which led to the cliff top, 250 feet up. In my eagerness I went up too fast. By the time I reached the top I was absolutely done, but Knight was even worse, gasping for breath like an untrained miler at the tape. I was exhausted myself, and my sodden battledress seemed to weigh a ton. My legs were leaden, my lungs bursting. I could hear the squeak and squelch of wet boots as the rest of the troop followed us up from the beach. Fortunately the night was warm.

I had an idea we were already behind schedule, and I led on between a few small houses. We had to be clear of Guernsey by 3 a.m. As we passed each house, a dog inside began to bark. Presently there was a chorus of barking dogs behind us.

"For God's sake, come on," I panted to Knight, who seemed to be slowing down. "We haven't got all night."

By then I had my second wind and didn't feel tired again during the operation. My headquarters party was close on my heels: Lieutenant Johnny Giles, C.S.M. Beesley, Knight, two lance-bombardiers and a sapper. Another dog began to bark.

"Shut up!" Johnny Giles yelled at it, and the barking became louder.

"This is going to alert the whole damn island," somebody remarked ruefully.

One of the staff officers in London had suggested sending an aeroplane to circle over our operational area with a view to deadening any noise we might make, and I had accepted this idea. At this moment I saw the aircraft, an Anson, circling above us at about three hundred feet. He was plainly visible and his exhaust pipes were glowing red.

The machine-gun post, which was the first objective of my little group, was at the tip of the Jerbourg Peninsula, eight hundred yards from the landing place. I went as far as the barracks with de Crespigny. Just before going into the barracks, de Crespigny broke into a house to get information from the householder. I went in with him through the back door. However, the man we found was so terrified that he had entirely lost the power of speech; all he could do was to let out a series of shrieks. We left de Crespigny and began climbing down the cliff. I sent Beesley, Knight and the others to the cable hut. Johnny Giles and I crawled up on either side of the little mound in which the machine-gun nest was dug. I carried grenades and a .45 Webley; Giles, a giant of well over six feet, had a tommy gun.

We jumped to our feet and into the nest, a sandbagged circle. We were both ready to shoot, but I found myself face to face with Johnny's tommy gun; and he with my Webley.

"Hell!" Johnny said bitterly, "there's no one here!"

We went down to where the others were cutting the cables leading from the hut. Knight asked me rather plaintively:

"Please can I blow the place up, sir?" He had a pack of demolition stores on his back and was aching to use it.

"No. Apparently the Germans don't know yet that we've come. There's no point in announcing it. Just cut the cables."

We went back to see if we could help de Crespigny's party. It was pitch dark, and as I approached, Corporal "Curly" Gimbert burst through a hedge at me. The next thing I felt was a bayonet pushing insistently through my tunic.

"Password!" Gimbert hissed.

He was a big, powerful man. It seemed a long time before I could say anything. There have been worse occasions since, when I've been less scared. At last I remembered the word and let it out with a sigh.

"Desmond!" I said.

Gimbert, recognising my voice, removed the bayonet quickly.

27

"All right, Colonel."

I thought he sounded disappointed.

When we rejoined de Crespigny, his men had finished searching the barracks. There, as in the case of our machine-gun nest, no one was at home. It was past time for the fireworks at the airfield between the Germans and our Independent Company. I listened. The night was still. Ignored, the dogs had stopped barking some time before. I looked at my watch and saw with surprise and some dismay that it was a quarter to three: time to go.

We formed up on the road between the barracks and the Doyle Column, a monument we had used as a landmark. It was easy to guess from the muttered curses that the others shared my disgust at our negative performance and at the fact that we had met no Germans. George Herbert was particularly upset and begged me to give them a few minutes more to visit some houses nearby which he thought might contain Germans. In this atmosphere of complete anti-climax, it was clear that none of us wanted to leave. But I called the officers together.

"We've got to be back on the beach in ten minutes," I said urgently.

They got their men going on the run. In short order, I herded them like a sheepdog down the concrete steps. Still the enemy showed no sign that he knew of our visit.

I was last down from the cliff top, with Peter Young clattering just ahead of me. Near the bottom I accelerated and suddenly realised that my feet had lost the rhythm of the steps. I tripped and tumbled the rest of the way, head over heels. I had been carrying my cocked revolver at the ready. During the fall it went off, seeming tremendously loud and echoing against the cliffs. This, at last, brought the Germans to life. Almost at once there was a line of tracer machine-gun fire from the top of the cliff on the other side of our cove. The tracers were going out to sea, towards the spot where I thought our launches must be awaiting us.

"You all right, Colonel?" It was Johnny Giles's anxious voice.

"Yes."

I told him to get on with forming the men up on the beach.

I had landed hard on the rocks and was shaken and bruised, but there was nothing seriously the matter. I never carried my pistol cocked again.

Within five minutes my men were all formed up on the beach. I knew now that we were late for our rendezvous—it was ten past three—and that if the destroyers had obeyed instructions they were already steaming towards Britain. I saw the dim shapes of our launches then, about a hundred yards out.

"Come in and pick us up!" I shouted.

"Too rough! We've already been bumping on the rocks. We'll stove our bottoms in if we come any nearer."

"Well, send your dinghy in for the weapons."

They did. It was a tiny craft, no more than nine feet in length. With each load of weapons went two or three men. As it came in for the fifth run, a high sea picked it up and smashed it against a rock. The dinghy was a total loss, and one trooper was reported drowned.

"The rest of you will have to swim for it," I ordered.

Fortunately we were equipped with Mae Wests and we all started to blow them up.

Some of the men began peeling off their uniforms and wading into the sea. Three men came up to me in the darkness. I recognised Corporal D. Dumper of Lieutenant Smales's road-block party.

"Could we have a word with you, please, sir?" Dumper said. He seemed a little nervous.

"What is it?"

"I know we should have reported this in Plymouth, sir," he said apologetically, "but the three of us are non-swimmers."

I was ready to explode. The original letter calling for Commando volunteers had specifically mentioned that they must be able to swim. Then I calmed down.

"I'm afraid there's nothing we can do for you except try to send a submarine to pick you up tomorrow night," I said. "You chaps hide up. Come back on the beach at two o'clock tomorrow morning and flash a torch."

"Thank you, sir," Dumper said. "Sorry to be such a nuisance."

I removed my tunic and struck out in the water. Some of

the men, with more wisdom than modesty, preferred to swim naked. I had the added handicap of sentiment. In my right hand I carried a silver cigarette case which my wife had given me; in my left, a spirit flask which had been my father's. A rough sea had come up since our original landing. In these circumstances the hundred yards to the launches seemed endless. For the first fifty, breakers thundered and broke over my head. It took, I suppose, seven or eight minutes to swim out, but it seemed hours and I was exhausted. As a sailor bent down from the launch to drag me aboard, the final effort of helping him, to my great annoyance, made me let go of the flask and case. When I was interested again in such matters, I noted that my wristwatch had stopped. I asked the time.

"Half-past three," the Captain said.

"My God! We'll have missed the destroyer completely."

The discipline and bearing of the men during the difficult swim out to the boats was admirable. There was no shouting or panic; each man swam along quietly. The crews of the launches were continually diving in to help the most exhausted men over the last stages of their journey. Altogether, this most difficult re-embarkation was carried out quietly and efficiently.

With dawn half an hour off, it looked as if we should have to head for home in the launches. This was not a prospect to bring delight. The crews of these boats were brave men, mostly yachtsmen with no service experience. At this point, they seemed unable to reach a decision for further action. The second launch had just broken down: ours threw it a line and had it in tow. There was a general discussion of the situation by all hands. Even the engine attendant left his recess to chip in.

"What the hell are we going to do now?" he demanded.

This was too much for me.

"For heaven's sake," I snapped, "let's stop the talking and pull out to sea."

They did as I suggested.

I was sure that by now the *Scimitar* had gone; a certainty shared by all aboard the launch. It now seemed doubtful that, towing the other launch, we could make it to England, even if we were lucky enough to escape German fighters which could easily nip out from airfields on the French coast. I felt that only a piece of extraordinary luck could save us.

"May I borrow your torch?" I asked our Captain.

He handed it to me, and I flashed it out to sea, knowing that this was a despairing hope.

To my delight, a series of answering flashes came back from just beyond the point. The *Scimitar's* Captain, I later learned, had decided to take one last sweep around for us on his way home! He was exposing himself to a tremendous risk of air attack, as daylight was only a few minutes off and the Luftwaffe had many airfields within a few minutes' flying time. Our own air cover of Hurricanes could not be expected at this time to operate so near to the coast of France.

After blowing up the ailing launch, we transferred to the destroyer.

Captain de Crespigny, noticing that I was shivering with cold, kindly lent me his tunic. I wore no shirt, and put the tunic directly over my bare shoulders and arms. Just before getting to Dartmouth, de Crespigny said:

"Oh, by the way, Colonel, I do hope everything will be all right."

"What do you mean?"

"I forgot to tell you that I've been suffering from scabies," he said.

I rushed off for a hot bath in the Captain's bathroom. Like the operation itself, nothing came of it. My own tunic, which had my name sewn into the collar, was picked up next morning by the Germans on the beach. Durnford is a well-known name in the Channel Islands and some of the Durnfords there were harried a good deal by the Gestapo who thought that I might still be lying up in the Island, harboured by namesakes.

We arrived back in Dartmouth, safe but distinctly down in the mouth, at eight in the morning.

It was not until then that I learned from Ronnie Tod what had happened to the Independent Company. Two of their launches, as already noted, had broken down before they reached the Channel Islands. That left them still with two boats. They were not as fortunate, however, as I had been in discovering that the de-gaussing had reversed the compasses. One of their remaining boats had landed blithely on Sark instead of on Guernsey. The other had run into a rock. No wonder I had failed to hear shooting from the direction of the airfield!

I put in an immediate request for a submarine to be sent to pick up Corporal Dumper and the other two non-swimmers. The authorities, however, declared that the aim was not worth the risk. All three became prisoners of war, together with the trooper who had been reported missing, presumed drowned, when the dinghy capsized. These four men were the first Commando soldiers to fall into the hands of the enemy. Since they remained prisoners until the end of the war, I feel sure they considered the honour a doubtful one. The prisoners behaved in the tradition which all Commando prisoners were to follow throughout the war. They collected all the equipment they could find on the beach and buried it. They then went into hiding, but in the limited area of Guernsey they were all discovered within two or three days. Despite a severe grilling from the Gestapo, they gave away no information whatsoever.

The raid was, of course, a ridiculous, almost a comic, failure. We had captured no prisoners. We had done no serious damage. We had caused no casualties to the enemy. Even the roll of barbed wire for Lieutenant Smales's road block had proved too heavy to lift up the steep steps. There had been no machine-gun nest and, to all practical purpose, no barracks. We had cut through three telegraph cables. A youth in his teens could have done the same.

On the credit side, we had gained a little experience and had learned some of the things *not* to do. It was very clear that we urgently needed good and reliable landing craft for such an operation. It was equally clear that two hours on shore was not long enough to accomplish any worthwhile aim.

Of course, the Prime Minister, whose promptings had largely initiated the Commando idea, had a complete report of the operation in a few hours. He didn't like it. He sent a strong directive to Headquarters Combined Operations.

"Let there be no more silly fiascos like those perpetrated at

Guernsey," he wrote. "The idea of working all these coasts up against us by pinprick raids is one to be strictly avoided."

Mr. Churchill was dead right. He meant that we should go about this Commando business properly, or not at all, and he told Lord Keyes, who was now Chief of Combined Operations, to plan some really worthwhile raids.

As for me, I was more than ever determined to mould a unit that would take any raid in its stride, and to bring back results. Only results mattered.

I knew now that I had a long way to go to achieve them.

Chapter III

LEARNING FROM MISTAKES

BACK in Plymouth, No. 3 Commando got down to really serious training, learning the lessons of our mistakes in Guernsey. We had acquired several naval cutters and two very large motor boats, the *Sweet Marie* and *Sweet Content*, which had been used in peacetime as pleasure cruisers in Plymouth Sound. With this fleet we carried out landings every day up and down the coast, with sea approaches of up to twenty miles. The boats were run and maintained entirely by our own men; sometimes in severe weather we had near escapes from being wrecked, but we had to take our chance of this sort of thing.

By mid-August we were expert at these landings, which were always followed by a battle on shore with the remainder of the Commando and re-embarkation under counter attack. The invasion scare was at its height and our arrival from the sea usually caused grave panic among the mothers and children enjoying themselves in the sun on the beach, even though we invariably sent an officer on ahead to warn them. At the same time, intensive training in musketry, weapon training and troop manœuvres was carried on, and the greatest attention was paid to discipline, marching and turn-out. Some of our early training schemes were very tough indeed, and I would have the Medical Officer present at the end of the exercises to examine all men for physical fitness. Anyone showing any signs of tiredness or other infirmities, was at once returned to his unit. By the end of August we had weeded out quite a number of unfit officers and men.

The naval authorities in Plymouth could not have been more helpful to us. Admiral Dunbar Nasmith gave us skilled seamanship instructors and every man was trained to be expert in boat-pulling and in all details of handling boats. We fitted the cutters out with sails and they were out in the Sound every evening. Also, whenever possible, we sent men out in minesweepers and patrol vessels from Dartmouth and Falmouth, so as to get them used to the atmosphere of the sea.

On the other hand, the military Command at Plymouth looked on us with suspicion and resentment. It was part of the 1940 mentality. The War Office regarded us as Winston Churchill's private army and wanted to abolish us. "Unnecessary, irregular, taking the best men," were the sort of phrases used. The Plymouth staff had the "hollow square" and "thin red line" outlook.

"What *is* all this nonsense about creeping about at night and slitting throats?" was their viewpoint.

They did not at all understand our activities. When we wanted a training area they would stall; under pressure, they would give in to us. Any disorder in the town was always put down to us. The pompous old-timers who for the most part made up the staff in Plymouth could not bear the thought of anything new such as our unit.

Admiral of the Fleet Lord Keyes came down in his capacity as Chief of Combined Operations, late in August, to see our training. We were able to show him a landing twenty miles from Plymouth, entirely organised by ourselves. We towed cutters behind the motor boats and proved to him that we had assimilated the naval technique of beaching the cutters in the heavy surf which was running that day. I had a wonderful day with Roger Keyes, which ended with a dinner party given by Admiral Dunbar Nasmith, the naval Commander-in-Chief at Plymouth. Before the dinner I told Admiral Keyes about the difficulties we had encountered with the military authorities.

One or two of these military authorities were at the dinner and he spoke to them in severe terms:

"Look here, if you don't help these Commandos, you're going to be most unpopular in high places."

This caused a slight improvement in the situation. Roger Keyes, when visiting No. 8 Commando a few days later, said to Colonel Bob Laycock commanding them:

"You want to go down and see No. 3 Commando. They've got their own boats and handle them like professional sailors."

Bob sent his second-in-command down to study our training methods soon afterwards.

In September, 1940, Roger Keyes developed a project for

the capture of the island of Pantelleria, an Italian island which lies in the Mediterranean not far from Malta. We called this operation, the "Shake-the-World" project, as Admiral Keyes was very fond of using this phrase. The Commando force was also, at short notice, to operate in the Atlantic; if the Germans should show signs of attacking any of the Atlantic islands our role was to forestall them by occupying these islands before the Germans could get there.

The Admiral decided to concentrate the bulk of his ten Commandos at the Combined Operations base situated at Inveraray in western Scotland, so that we could develop our training technique and rehearse the actual details of the attack on Pantelleria. No. 3 Commando left Plymouth thankfully; no one could have been kinder than the citizens of the town, and no one could have been more helpful than the Royal Navy, but the continual nagging and obstruction from the army authorities was really beginning to get us down.

The base at Inveraray was in a very incomplete state, but we settled down in the camp, determined to enjoy ourselves. The arrival of all these soldiers, mostly English, was not at first welcomed by the local inhabitants, who regarded it as another English invasion of their country. This attitude was soon broken down.

At Inveraray we made our first acquaintance with properly armoured assault landing craft. I had been pestering Admiral Keyes ever since Guernsey to let us start training in these craft. Obviously, he agreed. Our very first morning in Inveraray I had a message from him to the effect that two such craft were on the way to me for No. 3 Commando. With my officers and N.C.O.s, I rushed to the beach. We were just in time to see them coming in at about six knots, a big wave foaming at each square bow. They rode very low in the water and had no superstructure. I felt a glow of excitement as they came right up to the steep beach and lowered their ramps.

Johnny Giles wore a look of almost worshipful attention. None of us had ever before seen a proper landing craft.

"That's a lot better than we had for Guernsey," he muttered.

"They do look like the real thing," I said.

Now, I thought, we were ready to operate. Half an hour

after the two craft arrived I had each of them loaded, with thirty men and full equipment. At the time, a Commando troop consisted of forty-seven men and three officers. Our work became so identified with these assault craft that it was not long before we reformed our troops into sixty men and three officers. This meant that one troop would fit exactly into two landing craft. Just then, however, my principal concern was to practise landings. I insisted on from twenty to thirty each morning: and each morning Charlie Head would shout at the men until he was hoarse:

"Come on: you can do better than that!"

They *did* do better. Before we had finished we could empty a boat, with all weapons, and run to cover twenty-five yards away, in ten seconds. Algy Forrester's F Troop held the blue riband for that. Algy was determined to make his the best troop in the best unit in the world. Peter Young's H Troop, with a time of fourteen seconds, held the record for re-embarking.

The country round Inveraray was also ideal for our land training. There was a great stretch of uninhabited hilly country, with rivers and moors and the sea all nearby. Landings from the sea followed by long approach marches and difficult river crossings continued the process of eliminating the unfit. Throughout my five years of Commando work I never found a better method of spotting weaknesses except in the actual battle. Any officer or man who weakened or showed lack of humour was instantly dismissed.

I thought that we had found out all the weaknesses at Plymouth, but this tough life at Inveraray sorted out still more who could not take it. It really was a hard life. There was nothing to do but work. We would start on the landing craft at 8 a.m. and follow on with drill, marching, shooting and long schemes on the hills. We also went in for obstacle courses and close combat, which included wrestling and work with knives and pistols, taught by two ex-Shanghai policemen. We learnt methods of getting into houses, throwing grenades in front of us and shooting the tommy guns. A normal day would end at dark, but at least three times each week the men were out at night. I knew the importance of getting them good at night work. At first they were awkward and noisy, apt to lose their way. They gradually and steadily improved. All of us did many long night marches across the wild and trackless hills. In a month they weren't the same men; they could almost see in the dark. They were used to it and it had become a natural thing, and that was what I wanted.

All this was rather too much for one or two of the more elderly officers, and for some of the men. These were promptly returned to their units. One man, a good regular soldier, took to booze in order to fortify himself; this was a vicious circle and I had to get rid of him. I found that another officer had a vivid imagination and was telling people at Inveraray:

"I've been across the Channel half-a-dozen times. I shot up the German officers in the casino at Le Touquet."

He hadn't, nor had anybody else. I sent him off at once. I was always able to get good officers to replace those whom I had sent away.

Lieutenant Bill Lloyd was one of the best of these replacement officers. He was a very good-looking man, tall, well-built and dark, and looked fit and keen. I liked the fact that he was an Australian. I wanted to get a few Commonwealth men in; the idea appealed to me. I liked free-thinking, free-talking people. After interviewing Bill, I told him he was in, the decision being mine alone.

"Come to the mess and have a drink to celebrate your joining No. 3 Commando," I said to him.

"Mine's a pint," Bill said when we got to the mess.

I never heard him ask for anything else, he was never a man for half measures. I posted him to Algy Forrester's Troop to make sure he learned things the hard way, as Algy was my toughest disciplinarian. It worked out well and they became good friends.

They were both keen on rock climbing and began to work out a technique of landing on rocky beaches and climbing cliffs, instead of landing at the obvious places. Bill and Algy came to me one night, and Algy said:

"Look Colonel, this landing on the obvious beaches is a mug's game. The Germans will be waiting for us with machine guns. Bill and I have been working out a technique whereby we land at the most difficult place. Nobody will be expecting us at these sort of places and with good training we'll get ashore unopposed."

"There isn't much doing at the moment," I said to them. "Try out some of these rough landings and see how they work."

They went ahead; they tried rocky shores, then low cliffs, then high cliffs. Algy worked out a scheme whereby one man climbed the cliff with a rope, then he pulled up more ropes and anchored them on top of the cliff so that the other men could climb up. This needed one ace climber. At first Algy was the ace climber; then he trained Bill Lloyd, and between them they trained a good many others. It became an established and important part in our training and we used it to keep our distinguished visitors happy. It was highly spectacular, and it is the same thing exactly that the Royal Marines do to this day at the Royal Tournament and elsewhere. In addition to being good training, it was a wonderful thing for morale. A man who could climb a cliff got the feeling that he could do anything.

Roger Keyes was running into difficulties over his Pantelleria project, which was put off for a couple of months. We were moved into comfortable billets at Largs on the Clyde. Largs was excellent for our purpose. It was a holiday town for Glasgow, with plenty of accommodation in lodging houses and hotels. There was an enormous area of rough land behind the town where we could carry on with our training, using live ammunition. Continually, we endeavoured to make our training as near as possible to the real thing and to get everybody used to the noises of battle, to carrying the necessary loads, and to the landings and approach marches which would precede battles. Later on all this type of training was adopted for the battle training of the regular army. Everybody, down to private soldiers, was encouraged to submit ideas which we then tried out. Largs was a clean, prosperous-looking town and the officers and men were able to enjoy themselves in the evenings.

One day I received a War Office letter which stated that, from thence onward, the units were to be known not as Commandos but as Special Service Battalions. I thought it better to leave S.S. to the Germans. Fuming, I showed the letter to Charlie Head.

"Take no notice of this bloody thing!" I snorted. "Never let the term Special Service Battalion appear on any of our orders. We'll ignore these fools and soon get our right name back."

Charlie, always ready for a fight, grinned:

"That's the stuff, John: stick to your guns!"

A rather peculiar impasse resulted for a while. I kept getting letters from the War Office addressed to "Lieut. Col. J. Durnford-Slater, Officer Commanding A Company, Special Service Battalion." If one of these called for a reply, I would send a letter to the War Office signed "Lieut. Col. J. Durnford-Slater, Officer Commanding No. 3 Commando." Perhaps I was being stubborn, even a bit schoolboyish, but I won my point. Before many weeks, the War Office surrendered. We were No. 3 Commando, and no S.S. nonsense about it.

In December, 1940, Roger Keyes again got his Pantelleria project under way and three large merchantmen, the *Glen Gyle*, the *Glen Roy* and the *Glen Erne*, arrived in the Clyde. These were fine, big, fast ships, each carrying a dozen landing craft. We embarked in them at Gourock and sailed for the Isle of Arran for final training and rehearsals.

Finally, Admiral Keyes brought a party of eminent men to see our full-scale rehearsal, a landing by No. 3 Commando and No. 8 Commando, which was to take place near Brodrick, on the Isle of Arran. On the efficiency and dash of that rehearsal the fate of the project was to depend. Naturally, I was determined to make my part of the show a spectacular success.

On the night of the rehearsal I was put in charge of the officers and men aboard the *Glen Roy*. The high-ranking officers were to witness the landing from the beach. The orderly officer on board the *Glen Roy* was a capable young man, David Sutherland.

"Make sure to give us all a call at one o'clock," I told him.

The operation was to be manned at two.

Instead of going to the Officer of the Watch, Sutherland asked the guard commander—there were guard-room prisoners

40

aboard—to call him at one. Sutherland, like the rest of us, had been training all day. Everybody was dead tired.

I woke up in the dark of night with a terrible feeling that something was wrong. I switched on my cabin light and looked at my watch. It was 1.45 a.m.!

Horrified, I jumped out of my bunk and ran from cabin to cabin, waking as many of my officers as I could. They were all sound asleep and I had to give each one a thorough shake.

"Get up!" I roared. "We're late! We're due to land!"

When they seemed conscious I told them to get their men stirring.

Then, desperately, I ordered the landing craft to delay for ten minutes. That was the best I could do. There were three ships taking part in the rehearsal and there was a rather complicated action to be sychronised. Eventually the twelve landing craft left our ship—each only one-third manned. I groaned, looking back at the *Glen Roy* from about one hundred yards. Her rails were solidly lined with my late-rising men.

The craft struck the beach on schedule, but the landing came as an anti-climax for the big shots from the War Office. It must have been a sad and terrible blow for poor Admiral Keyes when he saw a mere thin trickle of men dash to shore when he expected a swarm.

Next day I apologised to him with heartfelt humility:

"I've let you down horribly," I said.

The size of the man was measured in his reply.

"You have," he said, "but you've had your lesson. Now this will never happen to you operationally where it could truly mean disaster."

Keyes had the reputation in the Navy of being a terrific martinet. To me he seemed the most reasonable and charming man on earth.

Another period of waiting followed, and at last we were told that Pantelleria was off. I am quite sure that this would have been easy meat for our Commandos, but the subsequent maintenance, feeding and defence against attack from the Luftwaffe and Italian air force would have been a very different matter. I believe that with a good Commando force most places can be captured; from time to time, for my own edification, I planned an attack on Heligoland, which I am convinced we could have taken, but the subsequent period would not have been much fun.

We were terribly disappointed about Pantelleria, but as we left for Largs to return to our billets there, Roger Keyes, who came to see us off, whispered to me:

"Don't worry, I've got another one up my sleeve for you. No. 3 Commando are my first choice and I will guarantee to have you in on it."

Chapter IV

LOFOTEN

ROGER KEYES kept his promise. A month later, in February, 1941, he sent me a signal to go to Troon the next day to meet one of his staff officers. I thought to myself, this is it.

Colonel Dudley Lister commanding No. 4 Commando, was also at the meeting. We adjourned to Dudley's bedroom at the Marine Hotel, Troon, as we wanted a quiet place to talk things over. The Admiral's staff officer said:

"Nos. 3 and 4 Commandos are going to carry out an attack on the Lofoten Islands in northern Norway. The object is primarily to destroy all the oil installations; secondly, to destroy shipping; and thirdly, to bring back prisoners, and volunteers for the Norwegian navy."

The code word for the operation was "Claymore" and it was primarily for the benefit of the Ministry of Economic Warfare. The plan called for a simultaneous attack on the key ports of the Lofoten Islands, Stamsund, Henningsvaer, Brettesnes, and Svolvaer, the capital. Fifty per cent of Norway's herring and cod oils were produced on these islands, and the oil was made into glycerine for explosives, and vitamins A and B for the use of the German army. In addition, vast quantities of fish, salt, chilled and fresh, were exported from the area to Germany.

The Lofotens, 850 miles from Scapa Flow, were well inside the Arctic Circle. It was up to the Royal Navy to get us there. At this season the temperature was expected to be below freezing. Snow would fall one day in every two. Gales would blow about every ten days. In January, three U-boats had been reported around the islands. Fortunately no aerodrome north of Trondheim was fit for operations in mid-winter, and the only air activity expected was by an unarmed reconnaissance JU52 which was known to patrol the area three times a week.

43

Intelligence reported only twenty German military personnel in the area. The local population were said to be anti-Nazi, but port officials were Germans and the mayor was a quisling. The four ports were connected by telegraph. A telephone cable joined them to Norway's mainland.

Late in February we boarded H.M.S. *Princess Beatrix* for Scapa, where we were to carry out final training before sailing for the operation. We were now organised in six troops instead of ten, so each troop was allotted two landing craft. H.M.S. *Princess Beatrix* carried six small landing craft and two large ones slung from the davits. The procedure before landing was that the davits swung out, boats were lowered to deck level and we then stepped into them and were lowered into the sea. The craft then ran on to the landing place under their own power.

By now we had made our plans. All the oil and fishing installations were to be blown up. We had trained plenty of our men as demolition experts. They were mad keen to get on with this job. The remainder of the Commando were to cover the demolition operations, arrest the Germans and quislings and to secure volunteers for the Norwegian navy. We had with us a number of Norwegians under Captain Martin Linge. He was a well-known leader of the Norwegian Resistance, and a number of the men under him had recently crossed from Norway in fishing boats.

Martin Linge was tall and slender with a little dark moustache. He didn't look like a Norwegian. He was delighted to be coming with us and asked me to tell him what his troops could do best to help the operation.

"I'd like them split into seven small parties," I said, "one to come with my headquarters, and one to go with each troop, to act as guides and interpreters. I'd like you to come with me to be my personal advisor."

He was a very alive, capable sort of fellow, the sort who would make a good Commando. His troops were well turned out and keen, confirming the impression that he was a good officer. I asked him about the factory owners:

"How would they like their factories being blown up?"

"Don't worry," he said, "if they are loyal Norwegians they will take it well; if they are not, what does it matter?"

We became firm friends. Charlie Head and I regarded him as part of the unit.

H.M.S. *Princess Beatrix* was a fast cross-channel steamer now in the hands of the Royal Navy. Her Captain was Commander Joe Brunton, a cheerful man with a magnificent black beard. No. 4 Commando were carried in the sister ship, *Princess Emma*, commanded by Commander Kershaw, the famous rugby-football international. No. 3 Commando was to take on the ports of Stamsund and Henningsvaer; and No. 4 Commando, Svolvaer and Brettesnes. The whole force was under the overall command of the Commander-in-Chief Home Fleet, and we had an ample covering force including H.M.S. *Nelson*, H.M.S. *King George V*, two cruisers and five destroyers. The submarine H.M.S. *Sunfish* was to go ahead to act as a navigational beacon.

We sailed at once for Scapa Flow and on arrival there carried out our final training and planning. We accustomed ourselves to the ships in which we were to work, and continually practised with the landing craft. Every sort of situation was envisaged, and the most thorough plans were made. There was a possibility that our five escorting destroyers might be forced into a naval action, and so would have to leave us on shore for a considerable time. This made it necessary for us to carry rations for each man for forty-eight hours, in order that we should be able to maintain ourselves on land for this period.

Commander Geoffrey Congreve was on board *Princess Beatrix*. He was acting as liaison officer for Roger Keyes. Like Joe Brunton, he was tall and dark with a black beard; his ambitions were to win the V.C. and the Grand National, and he had already ridden in two or three Nationals. As my ambitions were precisely the same, we got on very well. One day Congreve said to me:

"I'd like you to meet Lord Lovat. I understand he's keen to join the Commandos."

Lovat had not yet joined us and had come as a spectator on the operation.

I said I would be delighted to meet him but I warned Congreve that I had no vacancies in No. 3 Commando except in the rank of subaltern. I had made it a firm rule that all officers joining No. 3 Commando had to start as subalterns and I had no intention of making any exceptions.

Lovat came on board and over tea we had a talk. He was tall and handsome and full of life and fun. We just had a general talk and I brought up the point that we had no vacancies for captains. After tea he left. That same evening I heard that he had joined No. 4 Commando in the rank of captain, as a troop commander. I was delighted because I knew he would be a great asset to the Commando organisation.

The system of making all officers joining No. 3 Commando start their service in the rank of subaltern, sometimes caused me to miss star turns, such as Lord Lovat, but in other ways had much to recommend it. All officers serving in the Commando knew that they would not have new officers coming in and taking up the captains' vacancies. It was up to all our officers to compete for these vacancies and the best man won. Similarly, in the ranks, all newcomers had to start as private soldiers, whatever their previous rank. This again caused keen competition and everybody had their chance of becoming an N.C.O.

During the time we were at Scapa Flow, the navy did every possible thing to help us. I found it inspiring to live in an atmosphere of such complete co-operation. No. 3 Commando was affiliated to H.M.S. *King George V* and we frequently went on board for baths, cinemas and other amenities. Our men struck up a great friendship with the ship's company.

We sailed for the Lofotens on the first day of March, 1941. Our route was not direct but in the shape of a great semi-circle so that we could keep outside the German air cover.

Commander Anthony Kimmins was on board, acting as Press Relations Officer for the Admiralty. On our first night at sea he said, I think jokingly, to Joe Brunton, the Captain: "Would you like me to take a watch?"

Joe immediately replied, "Yes, middle watch, please," and Anthony Kimmins was on the bridge from midnight to 4 a.m., all the way there and all the way back.

The voyage started badly for me. I had always dreaded sea-sickness and, on the first day, managed to lose my breakfast. Joe Brunton, his bearded face full of sympathy, took me in hand firmly.

"Beginning now," he said, "every morning at eleven you will consume with me a couple of bottles of beer with some cheese and pickled onions."

I must have looked as I felt, for Joe's sympathy turned to severity.

"That," he added, "is an order."

What could I do but obey? Happily, I can report that Joe's remedy effected a total cure. I have had endless rough sea passages since then, always using the beer-cheese-onions treatment. Never from that first day to this have I suffered from sea-sickness.

The ship rolled heavily throughout our four-day journey, being designed for cross-channel work and not for the heavy seas met in these northern waters. I was worried at first as many of our soldiers suffered badly from sea-sickness, but they recovered quickly and nobody was too ill to operate. Although it was early March, the weather became wonderfully warm after passing into the Arctic Circle and on the last day before landing we were able to sit out in the sun on deck. Everything was ready for our landing and every detail had been practised.

We had with us local pilots who knew the Lofoten waters. With their help, we were duly delivered to our objective off Stamsund at four o'clock on the morning of March the 4th. The submarine *Sunfish* was in position to guide us. The weather was a little cloudy at first, but soon cleared. The Admiralty information regarding first light proved inaccurate, for instead of being pitch dark, as it should have been when we started our run in from the *Beatrix* in the landing craft, it was broad daylight. I was in the leading landing craft which was commanded by the Flotilla Leader, a Canadian. He was worried about it being daylight instead of dark.

"Will I give her the gun, Colonel?" he asked me.

Our slow speed in daylight seemed to be bothering him.

I shook my head.

We could not yet see the town as we approached the harbour mouth. Suddenly, hundreds of small fishing trawlers poured

47

out of the harbour. George Herbert, a corporal now, was beside me.

"There come the fishing boats, Colonel," he remarked, "dead on schedule."

Every officer and man had been given the information contained in the intelligence summary. The Flotilla Leader was still nervous about the daylight.

"How about giving her the gun now, Colonel?"

"No: we're doing nicely," I said. "Let the fishing boats get out of the way."

A destroyer fired a burst of tracer across the bows of the leading trawlers. The Captain didn't want them to go out to sea, he wanted them under control but clear of the entrance which was merely a hundred yards across at the neck. In a few minutes the Lofoten fishing boats, sizing up the situation, had all hoisted Norwegian flags, an act which the Germans had specifically forbidden, and their crews joined in a great cheer of welcome. I felt good about that.

"At least they seem to be on our side," George Herbert said.

It seemed as if our landings were going to be unopposed. At this moment, however, one of our destroyers, the *Somali* sighted an armed German trawler pulling away from the harbour. Suddenly, the sound of gunfire shattered the early morning.

The threatened resistance soon faded. The *Somali* put the trawler out of the fight, killing fourteen and wounding five of her crew of twenty-four. Meanwhile, we went on with our landing.

The craft I was in snuggled up to a fish jetty. I jumped eagerly ashore, followed by my men. Perhaps I was too eager: I fell at the first fence, a long, three-feet-high pile of frozen cods' heads. When I picked myself up, somewhat sheepishly, I looked up the main street of Stamsund. It was empty as air. Then, a moment later, someone appeared. It was the local postman, hurrying to greet us. He said something in Norwegian. I turned hopefully to Captain Martin Linge.

"Ask him if there are any German soldiers in the town," I said.

"He says no," Martin told me. "But there are Gestapo and German businessmen."

"Where are they?"

The postman, eager to help, used his hands excitedly while giving information. A police sergeant came up and interrupted him. They were both anxious to co-operate against the Germans. Between them they provided us with the addresses of all the Gestapo agents in the town. As each of my troops came along, I told them to go on to their planned objectives, the factories and installations to be demolished. The police sergeant was not content: he insisted on providing guides for them from his small force. I could see that Linge, who had not stepped on Norwegian soil for a long time, was keen to get around and talk to his own people.

"May I go into the town, Colonel?" he asked. "There isn't enough for me to do here."

"Go ahead, Martin," I agreed. "Just leave one of your men to interpret for me. Do what you can to keep things friendly and report to me from time to time and let me know how things are going on."

"Right!" he said, overjoyed.

The local police sergeant led my party to the police headquarters which was in his charge. The headquarters were in a long, low, wooden building facing the quay.

"Would you like to use this as your headquarters while you are in town?" the policeman asked hospitably.

"Thank you very much, it's just right." And I took over.

Everything was covered in deep snow. The town consisted of wooden houses and fish factories, these having large oil-storage tanks. There was a strong smell of fish, but because of the cold it was not objectionable. Behind the houses and the factories, a hill rose steeply to a height of several hundred feet. Everybody was cheerful and it felt very like an exercise.

Fifteen minutes later I was standing in the doorway when I saw Lofty King and Bill Chitty, both big men and unit military police, forcing a prisoner along between them. Each had one of his arms. Squealing his protests, he looked and sounded like a fat pig being taken to slaughter. He wore a dark civilian suit. Lofty King saw me and grinned.

"Here's your top Gestapo boy, Colonel. What do you want done with him?"

Behind this ill-matched trio trailed a gang of locals, men, women, children and dogs, jeering, barking, laughing in delight. The Gestapo chap was cursing balefully in German. You didn't have to understand the language to guess his feelings. I said:

"Put him on a landing craft and send him right off to the *Beatrix*."

The civilian police sergeant sighed, grinning.

"He's a bad swine," he declared happily. "I'm glad to see him go in good company."

I had sent some men off under Charlie Head to take over the telephone exchange. Charlie knew very little about such matters but was remarkable at improvisation. He reported back to me by civilian telephone in good voice.

"All ours," he announced.

Later I heard that Lieutenant R. L. J. Wills had also become involved in a communication problem. He went to the post office and sent off a telegram addressed to A. Hitler, Berlin. It read:

YOU SAID YOUR LAST SPEECH GERMAN TROOPS WOULD MEET THE ENGLISH WHEREVER THEY LANDED STOP WHERE ARE YOUR TROOPS? (signed) WILLS 2-LIEUT.

Charlie Head was soon back with me. While Johnny Giles filed his No. 3 Troop into a borrowed bus and set off in great heart for an oil factory on the outskirts of town, Charlie and I took a walk down the street. We visited Johannsen, the owner of the largest factory in the town and of a general store adjoining it. By now, demolitions had begun elsewhere. The explosions around us made the landing sound like a real battle, which, of course, it was not. The noise was to continue, together with smoke and flames, all day.

When Charlie and I arrived at the Johannsen factory, its owner, prosperous-looking, stout, grey-haired, was in the midst of a violent argument with Lieutenant Williams, a demolition officer.

"But I've never sold oil to the Germans!" Johannsen protested. "I'm pro-British."

It was obvious to me that none of the factory owners could have avoided working for the Germans, regardless of their personal wishes or feelings.

"Then to whom does the oil go?" I asked.

Unable to supply an answer, he merely stared at me.

"Blow the place up," I said to Williams.

Twenty minutes later the factory was gone.

During the preparations of the charge of explosives, I saw many Norwegians roaring with laughter. Others raided Johannsen's store and came out loaded with bags of flour. Once his factory was destroyed, Johannsen himself seemed readier to accept the loss and understand our aims. He told us of other factories which we had not yet destroyed. In fact, each factory owner seemed to take special pleasure in informing on rival owners. It didn't matter to me what they said or did. My orders were clear: blow up every oil factory.

Halfway through the demolitions, however, I decided it would save time and ill feeling all round if I explained our motives to all the owners. I had them assembled in the police station and stood up before them.

"I'm sorry to have to do this," I told them. "I know we are destroying your livelihood, but you must see that it is necessary. This oil has been going to the Germans and is used to bomb Britain." I paused, I hoped dramatically.

"You are not to work for the Germans any more," I said. "We will be back in a few months to check up on you."

At this point Bill Chitty, who had been standing behind me with his tommy gun cradled in his arms, accidentally let off a burst. To my dismay, the bullets splintered the floor between my feet. I turned to him.

"You want to be careful with those bloody things," I said. "They're dangerous."

I think the factory owners thought this was done intentionally, to highlight the act. At any rate, they seemed to take my message most seriously.

By noon, great billowing funnels of smoke were rising into the sky. There was a smell of burning oil mingled with that of fish.

We were scheduled to sail at one in the afternoon. Thus far, everything had gone like clockwork. I looked up, wondering what was keeping the Luftwaffe. My reports told me that all the planned demolitions had now been carried out. In fact, our affairs were running so smoothly that Commander Anthony Kimmins found life a little dull and went skiing on a steep, snow-covered hillside behind the town. In civilian life, Kimmins was a well-known film director, but he seemed to take as readily to war as he did to work in the studios.

A rum ration had been issued in the landing craft. Some of the men did not feel like rum at 5 a.m. and a considerable portion was left over. Hearing a disturbance at the quay, I went down to see what was happening. One of the sailors had got at the unconsumed portion of the rum and was now fighting drunk. We had him sent off to the *Beatrix*. I never again allowed the issue of a rum ration before an action; we always kept it to enjoy when we had done our work.

The carrying out of the demolitions called for a great degree of skill, as we had strict orders to cause no unnecessary damage or casualties. Exactly the right charge had to be put on to destroy the machinery, without blowing bits of concrete or steel all over the town. I went to see Lieutenant Williams at work on the cod meal factory. He had a gang of six of our demolition experts. Small charges of gun-cotton were placed on vital pieces of the machinery and touched off. The electrical plant was smashed with sledge hammers, and then the current was turned on to complete the wreckage. There were four large oil tanks outside the factory. Six-pound gun-cotton charges were placed against these and the fuses were lit. The explosion seemed very small, but in a very few minutes the oil caught on fire. Flames soared for hundreds of feet into the air, and as the wind was blowing in our direction, these flames curled over our heads in an alarming way. It was obvious that this factory would produce nothing more for a long time.

At noon, a large crowd of civilians began to assemble at the quay, mostly young men with a scattering of women. Earlier, I had instructed the police sergeant to circulate the information that I sought volunteers to serve with the free Norwegian forces in Britain. I had suggested that any young man so inclined should assemble on the quay. Now there were several hundred there, a cheerful, noisy and excited crowd. But we had room to take only 150 from Stamsund. I said to Charlie Head:

"Will you make the selection? For God's sake, don't take any women!"

"You know me, John. I wouldn't do a thing like that."

I left him to it, but returned at half-past twelve to check on his progress. The landing craft was packed. In it were about 150 men, and one girl. She was a lovely blonde in her early twenties. I give Charlie that much: he showed taste. The girl smiled trustingly up at me. Charlie, standing on the quay, saluted gravely.

"I've made the selection, Colonel. Shall I send them off?"

We had no orders about bringing women volunteers back and I had already had enough battles with Authority. I said:

"What's that woman doing there, Charlie? Have her turned off at once."

Charlie saluted. Without a word he went on board and took the girl off. She burst into tears. Charlie looked at me. I said nothing, feeling a heartless brute.

Before we left the quay-side, we distributed to the towns-people goodwill gifts which we had brought them from Britain: tea and coffee, which they lacked completely, and toys for the children. Delighted, they pressed on us in return gloves, sweaters, scarves.

Martin Linge was back at my side.

"Do you think the population took the raid well, Martin?" I asked.

He nodded. "All the good ones took it well. That's all that matters."

I left in the last craft. Now the whole town was on the quay, cheering continuously. As we moved out of the harbour I heard them suddenly become silent. Then, over the water, came the singing of the Norwegian National Anthem. I could hardly bear to leave.

On board *Princess Beatrix*, I met our senior Troop Commander, Sandy Ronald, who had dealt with the port of Hennignsvaer ably assisted by Commander Congreve. Their experiences had been similar to our own and complete success had been achieved. A signal came from H.M.S. *Princess Emma* to say that No. 4 Commando had also been successful. It had been very cold all day and it took us several minutes to thaw out. But at 2 p.m. our flotilla was under way for Scapa Flow. Heading away from Norway after a successful operation with the ship throbbing its heart out at twenty-four knots is a great feeling, especially with a couple of gins and a good lunch inside you.

I knew that the raid could hardly have been more successful. We had destroyed eighteen factories; had sunk twenty thousand tons of shipping in harbour; had sent nearly a million gallons of oil and petrol up in smoke. Throughout the Lofotens we had taken prisoner 216 Germans and sixty quislings. We had seized maps, code systems, valuable documents. We had carried off three hundred loyal Norwegians who volunteered to continue their country's fight from Britain. To win all this we had not lost a man.

As the coast faded out of sight a hostile reconnaisance aircraft circled the convoy, just out of range of the anti-aircraft guns; no doubt it was calling up any U-boats within range. I went to see the first signal being despatched to the Admiralty in London. The naval signaller despatched a fifty-word message, briefly describing the successful operation, but at this distance transmission was bad. At the end of the message the Admiralty replied, "Repeat groups three to forty-seven." As the transmission of messages was giving our position away we gave up the effort for the time being.

The passage to Scapa Flow was uneventful. At Scapa we disembarked the prisoners, and recruits for the Norwegian navy. We also said goodbye to Commander Congreve. He was killed by a stray bullet in a cross-channel raid three weeks later. He could never bear to miss any action.

From Scapa Flow the *Princess Beatrix* took us on to Gourock where we disembarked. Roger Keyes was there to meet us and was delighted with our success. He promised me more action in the near future.

On the home front the Press shouted the story. The people talked of it in tones of pride. Even German radio grudgingly had to praise the secrecy with which the raid had been mounted and the complete success of its execution.

LOFOTEN

No. 3 Commando was granted a week's leave to celebrate our success. I set off from Largs with Charlie Head. In Glasgow we joined separate parties, and I told Charlie to fix up the sleepers on the train to London. Half-an-hour before the train was due to leave, I arrived on the station, rather tired, looking forward to stepping into my sleeper and going straight to bed. I saw Charlie escorting a girl named Betty up the platform, and asked him whether the sleepers were fixed up. He told me in so many words that he couldn't care less. A short, sharp altercation followed, and I went to find the sleepers, leaving Charlie to his self-appointed duty.

I found that a soldier from another unit, who had drunk a good deal, was in occupation of my sleeper. He refused to leave. I summoned the authorities and at length the soldier was ejected, after vomiting freely on my bed.

All this time a furious argument was going on between Charlie and myself, as Charlie said I had insulted his girl-friend. Two stalwart women railway cleaners appeared and started cleaning out the compartment. One of these could stand our argument no longer and closed it with the words:

"Betty this, and Betty that; ha' done wi' your Betty and let's get on with the work."

Charlie and I dissolved into helpless laughter and our only serious disagreement over thirteen years was instantly forgotten.

Chapter V

LARGS

EVERYONE had enjoyed the Lofoten raid and felt that they had done useful work, yet they were disappointed at not seeing more action. All ranks had a burning desire to get at the enemy, and on our return from leave we settled down to work even harder at our training so as to be absolutely ready at any time when we might be called to take on the best that the Germans could offer.

The American Embassy in London had, of course, heard of our job in the Lofotens. The United States was not yet in the war, but they knew they might be some day. For this reason the Embassy sent forty carefully-chosen American marines to live and train with us for some weeks. We were to teach them, as a sort of reverse lend-lease, our latest ideas. The U.S. Marines soon won all our shooting competitions and decided that our men were similar in outlook to themselves. We got along beautifully.

It was American policy at this time that none of these marines, training with us at Largs, should marry a British girl. Why, I haven't the least idea. But I was told of the ban.

Unfortunately, for the Embassy's peace of mind, there were many attractive Scottish girls in the town. It was not long before one very tall, good-looking marine began to show that he was seriously attracted towards a quiet and charming local girl who dressed well and carried herself with a kind of unconscious pride. For these reasons she was known as "the Duchess." On the other hand, the marine answered to "Texas."

The American intelligence system was most efficient and as the romance between Texas and the Duchess progressed, the Embassy kept telephoning me anxiously from London.

"Have they approached a parson?" the Embassy spokesman asked.

"Not as far as I know."

They kept ringing two or three times a day. Apparently the matter was of the utmost importance to the Embassy. I sent for Texas.

"I don't like enquiring into your private affairs," I said, "but your Embassy has asked me to find out if you intend to marry the girl."

"Yeah. I do. What of it?"

"*I* certainly have no objection," I hastened to respond. "I think she's a very nice girl. But your Embassy has this policy and on orders I must report the circumstances to them."

"Okay, Colonel," Texas said. "I understand your position."

But he obviously intended to carry the romance as far as the altar.

Finally an American colonel arrived from London to look into the matter personally. Evidently he decided that drastic action was called for. Next day Texas was shipped back to the United States.

In the Spring of 1941 many operations were prepared as it was thought that a move by the Germans against the Azores or Spain was imminent. The role of the Commandos was to forestall any such move. In May, 1941, the position became particularly dangerous and we were ordered to Inveraray so as to be ready to sail instantly if we were needed.

The planning of these operations was of great interest. I always endeavoured to put myself in the place of the enemy, and the time and place of our landings was always planned so as to come at the most inconvenient time, probably just before first light, and at an unexpected place. Landing craft were still in short supply and we had to practice with any boats we could get hold of. I had managed to get the cutters from Plymouth sent up by rail.

When we moved to Inveraray I called for volunteers to sail these cutters the eighty-mile passage. Four cutters eventually turned up safely, though many of the men looked distinctly haggard, as a gale had blown up and they had had a two-day passage in these open boats. The fifth cutter was wrecked on the Isle of Bute, but its occupants suffered no ill effects. They made their way to Inveraray in the customary manner of Commando soldiers without making any fuss.

A week later His Majesty King George VI came to Inveraray to inspect our training. There were many other units training at Inveraray and his programme had got behind time before he reached No. 3 Commando. The King arrived in a landing craft, looking very angry at the delay. The admiral and general accompanying him were sharply reprimanded for the unpunctuality. This was to my great advantage, as during the King's half-hour with No. 3 Commando I was left almost alone with him as generals and admirals kept well in the background. My first impression, after noting the King's intense dislike of unpunctuality, was of his youthful appearance and extreme interest in all our doings. Algy Forrester and Bill Lloyd put on a very fine cliff-climbing display, and we then showed His Majesty our landing technique, whereby the Commanding Officer always landed first and the troops followed at the double up the beach.

The operation eventually fizzled out, however, and we returned to Largs, disappointed.

It was just after this that Charlie Head got to hear that there were some good men at the Commando Replacement Depot at Achnacarry, near Fort William. We could always use good men. The Depot was not at that time in a state of advanced development and it was a case of the first C.O. to arrive taking away with him whatever men he wanted. I arranged for a car at six the next morning to take Charlie and myself to Achnacarry. Charlie had a wonderful ear for the military bush telegraph and reported to me that Dudley Lister, commanding No. 4 Commando, was also due in Achnacarry on the morrow for the same purpose.

Arriving in Achnacarry early next morning, I reckoned we had an hour's advantage over Lister. Charlie and I went to the parade ground where the available men were drawn up. I recognised the drill instructor as a man who had previously been in No. 3 Commando.

"What are these fellows like?" I asked him.

"They're a mixture," he said. "Most of them will make it, but some of them need a lot more training."

"Dismiss the men," I said. "Have them on parade again in half an hour's time, half of them in best battledress being drilled, the other half in their oldest clothes doing a training scheme. Make sure they're not doing it too well."

I asked him to put his best men on the lackadaisical training scheme.

Dudley Lister, a tall, aristocratic-looking officer, who had at one time been amateur heavyweight champion of Great Britain, arrived, exactly as I had expected, an hour after us. We greeted one another effusively.

"I suggest we share the men out, Dudley," I said. "We're pretty well off in No. 3, you take first choice."

Dudley fell for this. Naturally, he selected the smart-looking squad doing the drill. I took the others gleefully.

We spent the rest of the day watching training and enjoying ourselves. Soon after dinner I felt tired and went to bed. Dudley, a lively man, entertained the whole mess with his brilliant talk for another couple of hours. The Adjutant of the Depot had been away during the day and was not aware that Charlie Head belonged to No. 3 Commando. At last Dudley went to his quarters.

"What a difference between the two Colonels," the Adjutant remarked to Charlie. "One goes to bed at eight, the other keeps us roaring with laughter."

He seemed to be under the impression that Dudley always got his own way. Nevertheless, Dudley and I were always the best of friends. We just never did have any scruples about pulling a fast one on each other.

We were continually disappointed in the matter of operations, which kept appearing and then being abandoned, but our time was by no means wasted. There was always plenty more to learn.

Jack Churchill had been appointed my second-in-command. Commonly known as "Mad Jack," he continually evolved new and very unusual ideas for training. I gave all the troop commanders a pretty free run at this time as the great thing was to avoid boredom. Peter Young continued to study his troop attack and I often went and worked with his troop. Their technique had come on a lot since the Plymouth days and I found work in one of his movement groups the hardest exercise I have ever taken.

Another of Peter Young's activities was the training of potential N.C.O.s. I frequently took him off all other duties for this purpose, giving him a squad of about twenty-five promising men. They would do an intensive three-week course, after which Peter could tell me with almost unfailing accuracy which men would make good N.C.O.s and which would be just ordinary, good, private soldiers.

For some time Charlie Head and I were billeted in great comfort at Kelburn Castle, near Largs, the home of the Earl and Countess of Glasgow. Our host was wonderfully kind to us.

"I wish I were serving with you chaps," he would say wistfully.

He was about sixty years of age.

Lord Glasgow put his whole estate at our disposal and followed our doings with the greatest interest. Exercises with live ammunition were continually held but I do not think this disturbed the grouse unduly. Very occasionally we were able to return all his kindnesses in a small measure by providing some beaters for the grouse shooting.

Lord Glasgow was more than kind about asking us to shoot, and although Charlie Head and I were indifferent shots, he reserved his best days for the occasions on which we were able to come out. On one occasion when the Lord Chief Justice, Lord Caldecote, was staying in the house, Lord Glasgow told him that as we could not come out the next day, he could only have one of the lesser day's shooting.

"Sorry, Tom," he said, "but I must keep the best days for the soldiers."

Because of his kindness I found it an embarrassment when, very occasionally, some individual activity from within the ranks of No. 3 Commando seemed to repay his lordship with ingratitude. I always left Charlie to deal with such errors.

One day, when we were leaving for the office after luncheon, I heard Lord Glasgow calling in a loud voice:

"Head! Head!"

I jumped into a truck and told Charlie to settle what I sensed to be some trouble. Lord Glasgow called Charlie into his study.

"Some eggs have been taken from the chicken house in the garden," he said, and produced a clue which had been picked up there.

It was a bit of paper with "COMO 6" written on it. This happened to be the code name for No. 6 Troop, 3 Commando. Charlie was aware that a signal scheme had taken place that morning in the castle grounds and, thinking quickly, blurted:

"That must be the code for No. 6 Commando, sir. I'll get in touch with them right away!"

Lord Glasgow never did hear any more of this, but the culprits from 6 Troop did. They were duly punished. Charlie had no difficulty finding them. There were only four signallers in each troop.

One day, Lord Glasgow remarked that he ought to have a sixty-foot Scotch pine in the garden cut down. It was old, and possibly dangerous. Charlie Head was present and suggested that the unit's demolition experts would gladly blow the tree down.

"Could you do it without damaging any of my valuable shrubs?" Lord Glasgow asked. Charlie snorted.

"Our experts could drop it within six inches of a given position," he said.

I agreed that this would not only help our host but also provide good training for our troops. Next morning our demolition men cut a V into the giant tree and packed it with explosives. When the time came to lay the gelignite, two demolition officers argued as to the amount needed. They finally agreed, but I thought with Charlie that they had set too small an amount. A failure was unthinkable. Accordingly, Charlie sneaked out during lunch and added a quantity of explosive to that already planted in the tree. He also added detonators and the Bickford fuse.

After lunch, Lord and Lady Glasgow with several guests strolled out on the lawn to witness the expert job of demolition. They stood back some distance from the tree while Charlie and I lit the fuse, a simple job for an expert but demanding an entire box of matches from us. We ran back to the others. The fuse, which Charlie had made much too long, seemed to take hours to burn through. Then, with the loudest bang I had ever heard, the pine went sailing in clouds of black smoke at least forty feet in the air. It fell with a crash right into Lord Glasgow's prize shrubs. The force of the explosion had knocked us all, the Earl and his wife, their guests, Charlie and myself, flat on the ground. As we picked ourselves up we could hear the tinkling of glass. A moment later one of the maids came running out.

"My Lord! My Lord! The windows are broken!"

The situation was too much for me. I turned to my brother officer.

"I must get back to the office, Charlie," I said, trying to sound calm. "Just clean up here, will you?"

He did. The final count of smashed panes of glass was 132. Glass was scarce in those days, but as a scrounger Charlie had no equal. He managed to replace every one.

Again, in the summer of 1941, the Germans showed signs of a move towards the Atlantic islands, which they needed so badly as U-boat bases. This time the force appointed to forestall them consisted of the 1st Guards Brigade with No. 3 Commando attached. We thoroughly enjoyed working with the Guards. Their method of organising things was entirely to our liking; orders were clear and simple and they worked hard and played hard like our men. I borrowed six drill sergeants from them and allotted one to each troop, as I set great store by good drill. After a fortnight our men were drilling like guardsmen. In return, Colonel Dick Colvin, who was in command of the 3rd Grenadiers to whom we were attached, was kind enough to say that we taught them a great deal about movement across country, street fighting and a good many of the other arts of war.

We held a full-dress rehearsal of our projected operation; and as I was watching the exercise with Colonel Colvin, two Grenadiers were lying behind a wall while a section of No. 3 Commando, acting as the enemy, approached from the other side. Colonel Colvin said to one of the Guardsmen:

"What are you going to do now?"

The corporal was a little nonplussed in the presence of his Colonel. Colonel Colvin said:

"What's on your cap badge? Throw a —— grenade."

The good liaison went right through from the level of the private soldiers up to that of the Commanding Officers.

Again the operation was cancelled and action seemed a long way off. The one thing to do was to keep everyone in good spirits and keen. We went in for every kind of sport and produced an unbeatable boxing team. Johnny Dowling was a formidable lightweight, and as we had men of similar calibre to fill all weights, we never lost a match in army boxing. The Glasgow boxing promoters got to hear of this and many of our men were offered engagements for considerable sums of money. In the end I had to stop this boxing in Glasgow as the usual practice was to match our men with professionals of a slightly higher standard. The promoters knew that our men would fight to the last against a superior opponent, thus producing a blood bath which was pleasing to the spectators but apt to make the boxers punch drunk. We also produced first-class teams at both kinds of football.

The training in cliff climbing was carried to a more expert level and parties went frequently to Glencoe and other places in northern Scotland where really formidable cliffs were to be met with.

Added to this we had fairly frequent periods of leave. Some of these were official periods granted by Brigadier Charles Haydon, our Brigade Commander, but I was not always satisfied that these periods came sufficiently often and used to add unauthorised weeks of leave granted by myself. As I knew that Brigadier Haydon often motored through Largs, I always took the precaution of leaving one troop behind, telling the troop commander concerned that he was to have his men nicely turned out walking around the streets ready to salute the Brigadier's car very smartly at such times as he might think it was likely to pass through. Bob Clements, commanding No. 2 Troop, carried this off brilliantly one day; when I got back from an unauthorised leave period Charles Haydon told me how pleased he had been to see our men looking so smart and saluting so well as he passed through Largs. The whole Commando, less Clements's Troop, had been on leave on the day in question.

I knew that we had really reached a limit in our training and my one idea was to keep everybody happy and keen. From start to finish No. 3 Commando was a happy unit and the period in Largs contributed to this. The people were most friendly and helpful, and a good many of our men got themselves married to the pretty girls they met there. In spite of the frustration of not operating, I knew that the training had been valuable and that we had a really fine unit.

On the whole the other Commandos had been even more unlucky than ourselves in the matter of cancelled operations, and sometimes it was thought that No. 3 Commando were being specially favoured by Roger Keyes and others. One commanding officer, known as "The Old Man of Lamlash Bay" because of his long sojourn at Lamlash in Arran, worked himself into a great state of indignation on this score. He travelled to London, dressed himself up in full operation order, complete with tommy gun, fighting knife and other weapons and after having a few drinks presented himself in this attire in front of the immaculate Brigadier Charles Haydon at Combined Operations Headquarters, saying:

"I'm ready. Give me an operation."

The standard of behaviour in off-duty hours was always very high, but when you have five hundred high-spirited young men, full of life and good humour, kept waiting months for an operation, there has to be an occasional incident. Our internal police organisation was directed by Sergeant Bill Chitty, a good heavyweight boxer and a member of the police force before the war. We gave him half a dozen tough characters, including Lofty King, and told him there was to be no misbehaviour in Largs. If anyone did misbehave, Chitty and his men gave them a good handling and on the whole this was sufficient punishment without bringing the man up to the office in the morning.

Very occasionally an offence would be serious enough to warrant bringing the man before me. In these cases our police usually added an additional charge of assaulting the military police. This taught everybody to be extremely careful not to misbehave, but I must admit that sometimes my conscience was a little troubled when a man, escorted by King and Chitty, appeared before me with a couple of black eyes, charged with assaulting the unit police.

However, the proof of the system was its success; No. 3 Commando liked and expected it and invariably in every town where we were billeted relations with the police and civic authorities were of the very best. Men on leave from neighbouring units did not always understand or appreciate this treatment, however, and I had to deal with some awkward situations after Chitty and King had applied their strong-arm act on some of these visitors. When a man appeared in my office my practice was to do one of three things: he was either returned forthwith to his unit; given the maximum sentence in my power; or entirely discharged. We did not believe in petty punishment.

The No. 3 Commando police got on very well with the civil police force in Largs, especially after one incident in which Lofty King was involved. Outside Largs there were about fifty workmen, mostly from Ireland, who were doing the rough work on a large new reservoir just outside the town. They drew big money and came into Largs once a week to spend it all on liquor. For weeks they caused minor disturbances in which King and Chitty always acted with the civilian police. Then one Saturday the Irishmen started a real riot at the bus station, where the bus conductress had refused to let them on to the bus as they were too drunk. They jumped on to the bus and threw the conductress off, compelling the driver to drive them back to their huts by the reservoir.

The civilian police sent a message to King and Chitty for help, as the situation was out of hand. Bottles had been broken over heads, windows smashed, and the bus conductress was badly bruised. This was right up King's street. He quickly gathered up a few of our troops and commandeered another bus which was driven out to the camp. With King and Chitty in the lead, they went through the camp hut by hut and gave the belligerent Irish a severe beating. In the morning I had heard nothing of this until I received a call from the Superintendent of Police.

"Colonel, I want to thank you for the wonderful job your chaps did last night," he said.

Later I called for King and asked:

"What's all this about?"

"It's those Irish again," Lofty said. "We gave them a real

beating up last night. It's one of the best evenings I have ever had."

The Irishmen kept well clear of Largs after this.

Headquarters, Scottish Command, prompted by the War Office, made a new attack on our billeting system. The General Commanding said that householders were complaining bitterly about the extra work involved and of the difficulty of feeding the men. I arranged that officers should visit every householder in Largs who was billeting men and should make a written report on the attitude of these ladies. The universal attitude towards the Commando turned out to be one of pride and interest in all its doings. "Nae bother at all," was the usual comment.

At the same time I checked the reactions of Mr. George S. Thompson, manager of the Moorings Ballroom, where dancing took place almost every night. He wrote to me saying that neither he nor his patrons had ever made one single complaint about our men and that on innumerable occasions he had heard very complimentary remarks about their behaviour. I had taken my own steps to check this previously and had told two of my unit police to keep an eye on things. Later I was told that they interpreted this literally and said to the owner of the Moorings:

"The C.O. is watching your place a bit. We are willing to look after it for you to see no trouble arises."

Apparently they received a little protection money, although Mr. Thompson never spoke of this.

At about this time I perpetrated the most frightful indiscretion, which, fortunately, never came to light. We often had signal schemes, and Charlie and I thought it would add zest to our training if we reported the movements of all shipping on the Clyde on the unit wireless sets, which had a radius of only a few miles. Our signallers did this very efficiently from vantage points on the hills and neighbouring islands. Two days later I was horrified to receive a general warning, addressed to units all over Britain, that the material put out over our type of wireless set was capable of being picked up by powerful German receivers. We had reported the movement of three large convoys. Naturally, I was more than worried.

Next day Charlie and I called round at the Gourock Naval Operations Room. After a while, very casually, I asked:
"Any sinkings today?"

There were none. I restrained a tremendous sigh of relief. For the next several days we did the same thing. No sinkings, was the report. Finally, we were able to breathe again. I think if we had been discovered, it would have meant a court martial and dismissal from our appointments. In that case, I should have missed some of the best adventures of the war.

During the whole of our time at Largs, No. 3 Commando used to attach parties to the Royal Navy for duties on Atlantic convoy and anti-submarine work. This gave our men operational experience and I think was generally welcome to the navy, who soon found that the Commandos could be trusted with important duties.

On one occasion a party of one officer and fourteen of our men under a naval sub-lieutenant, brought back from mid-Atlantic the tanker *Sangro*, thirteen thousand tons, which had been found derelict and on fire. The tanker was safely berthed in the Clyde.

Our soldiers were landed in many strange places during these episodes. I remember a military police report coming in from Iceland, saying that a man named Drain had been walking along a quay near the main port of Iceland without wearing leggings. I refrained from taking the disciplinary action asked for in this report.

One night in the Victoria Hotel, Largs, I was drinking beer with three of our officers, Lieutenant Ruxton, Captain Bradley and Captain Sam Corry, our doctor. All three were Irish, and Buck Ruxton, who had been out on Atlantic patrols, was fuming over recent sinkings.

"I'm convinced," he said, "that the information comes from Ireland. What would you think of six of us taking leave to Dublin and blowing up the German Embassy?"

Things were very quiet just then and the idea attracted me. Six months had gone by since Lofoten and there was nothing else in sight. Lofty King and Charlie Head were to come with us to carry the explosives and we started detailed planning. At this stage of the evening I ordered that the project should be turned from the level of public-house conversation to that of a meeting in my office the next morning. Everybody was sworn to secrecy. Next morning we went further into the matter. The main difficulty was the removal of the Irish employees at the Embassy. Our Irish officers were confident they could do this, by offering them bottles of whisky and other rewards. It was arranged for Buck Ruxton and Sam Corry to go on leave that same day to carry out the necessary reconnaissance. They both assured me they could easily do this, travelling to Dublin in plain clothes. Charlie Head was to arrange the most careful alibis for all of us. The operation would have gone ahead and succeeded, but by good fortune the Vaagso project came up that same week so our efforts were diverted to more legitimate forms of warfare.

CHAPTER VI

VAAGSO

THE DAY after our discussion about the German Embassy project I received a telephone message requesting me to go at once to London and report to the Chief of Combined Operations. It was late in November, 1941. Admiral Mountbatten had taken over the command of Combined Operations from Admiral Keyes.

On arrival at Combined Operations Headquarters I was shown a very complete intelligence summary covering the area of Vaagso and Maaloy. I was told to study this summary before seeing Admiral Mountbatten. After reading it I was to be prepared to advise the Admiral as to whether No. 3 Commando could carry out a raid on Vaagso.

Vaagso is a town lying near the point of Norway nearest to the Shetland Islands, guarding the entrance to an important system of Norwegian fjords. There was a German naval anchorage there, strongly guarded by a battery of coastal defence guns, and there was a garrison of two hundred regular German troops. There were two other coastal defence batteries within a few miles. There were various anti-aircraft guns and a two-tube torpedo battery covered the entrance to the fjord. Four squadrons of Messerschmidts were within flying range, and a few German destroyers and motor-torpedo-boats were stationed in the area. I made a careful study of all these details and came to the conclusion that the operation could be carried out.

Very soon I was shown in to Admiral Mountbatten. At first he was a little doubtful about the project. It was to be the first Commando operation under his responsibility and I had the feeling that he wanted to be as positive as he could be of an initial success.

"This seems very ambitious," he said. "Don't you think it would be better to take on something not quite so strong? How do you intend to deal with the battery?"

I said: "If you will allow the cruiser *Kenya* and her attendant destroyers to come right up to three thousand yards and give the battery a real pounding at first light, I am sure that problem will be disposed of. You can rely on our men to look after the German garrison."

I had been told that the *Kenya* and four destroyers would be available and I was quite confident that after all our training and with our very fine men, we could do the job.

Mountbatten nodded. He never mentioned again the question of not taking the task on. He became, in fact, most enthusiastic. Knowing that it was desperately important at that stage of the war to have a success, he had just wanted to be convinced.

Broadly, our plan was for No. 3 Commando, supported by two troops of No. 2 Commando, to land at Vaagso and on Maaloy Island. All installations working for the Germans were to be blown sky-high. The German garrison was to be liquidated or captured and brought back to Britain together with certain Norwegian quislings. As in the Lofoten raid, a limited number of loyal Norwegian volunteers were to be taken off with us. We were to be carried in H.M.S. *Prince Charles* and H.M.S. *Prince Leopold*, two cross-channel steamers which had belonged to the Belgians and had been taken over by the Royal Navy and fitted with landing craft. Admiral Sir John Tovey, Commander-in-Chief Home Fleet, was to be in overall command. Admiral Burrough, flying his flag in H.M.S. *Kenya*, was to be our immediate naval Commander, and Brigadier Charles Haydon was to be overall military Commander. The Brigadier was to control matters from H.M.S. *Kenya* and I was to command everything on shore.

This venture, it was obvious from the beginning, was different in every respect from the Lofoten expedition. It was an ambitious project against a defended area and undoubtedly there would be a violent enemy reaction. At long last we would learn if our training had made us the fighting and killing force we were intended to be.

Brigadier Haydon was away at the time on another operation, so I was left on my own to do the planning with the naval and R.A.F. representatives. I liked it this way; it was much more

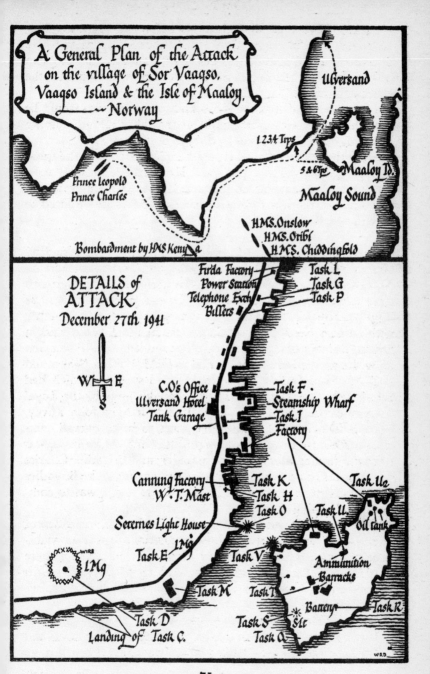

A General Plan of the Attack on the village of Sor Vaagso, Vaagso Island & the Isle of Maaloy, Norway

Ulversand

1.2.3.4 Tps

5 & 6 Tps

Maaloy Id.

Maaloy Sound

Prince Leopold
Prince Charles

H.M.S. Onslow
H.M.S. Oribi
H.M.S. Chiddingfold

Bombardment by H.M.S. Kenya

DETAILS of ATTACK
December 27th 1941

Firda Factory
Power Station
Telephone Exch.
Billets

Task L
Task G
Task P

W ✦ E
S

C.O's Office
Ulversand Hotel
Tank Garage

Task F
Steamship Wharf
Task I
Factory

Task Uz

Cannung Factory
W. T. Mast

Task K
Task H
Task O

Task U

Oil tank

Severnes Light House

1 Mg

Task E

XXXX WIRE
1 Mg

Task V

Ammunition
Barracks

Task M

Task T

Battery

Task R

Task D
Landing of Task C.

Task S

Task Q

W.R.D.

71

satisfactory to do your own planning and gave me greater confidence.

We started detailed planning directly I left Admiral Mount-batten's room. Charlie Head was with me as Signals Officer and I told him to make the signals plan. Charlie was soon deeply involved with the very high-powered naval signals officers. He did not know the first thing, technically, about signalling, but with his terrific personality and common sense was always able to get the results. I shuddered a bit when I heard him talking to the highly-trained naval officers about kilocycles and similar things, knowing that he had not the least idea what they meant, but very soon he got himself appointed chairman of the signals planning committee and left the others to do the talking, while he merely saw that things were kept on a commonsense level. I was quite confident that the signals plan would work.

After two days' hard work Charlie and I were satisfied with our planning and left for Largs to start briefing No. 3 Commando. A complete scale model of Vaagso had been made up from photographs. This showed every house and building and was of the greatest value. No place names were shown on the model, so that we were able to start using it at once for briefing.

We left Combined Operations Headquarters carrying the model in a large packing case, which was too big to go into a railway sleeping compartment. Instead, we had a first-class carriage reserved for us. About midnight, half-way to Scotland, a sailor who had drunk a good deal burst into the carriage and asked us to join him in a game of cards. Otherwise the journey passed without incident.

After giving Jack Churchill, my second-in-command, a brief outline of the operation, without mentioning any place names, I left for Scapa Flow to complete the naval planning with Admiral Burrough and Admiral Sir John Tovey. It was our invariable practice to keep place names secret until after the ships had sailed. Jack Churchill had all the information he needed to get on with the training, and I believe then, as now, that the fewer people in possession of vital information, such as place names, the greater the chance of achieving surprise.

At Scapa Flow I was met by Admiral Tovey's barge and taken straight off to H.M.S. *King George V*, the flagship. First

I had a long talk with Commodore Brind, the Admiral's Chief-of-Staff. In general, he agreed with my planning. Next, I was taken in to see Admiral Tovey.

The landing place I had chosen was a rough, rocky shore leading to a low cliff. It was just the sort of landing place Algy Forrester's system of rope climbing had prepared us to use. Admiral Tovey was not aware of our skill in this comparatively new technique.

"This is no good, Slater," he said. "It's no sort of place to land troops."

He suggested a little cove, which would be easier, some distance along the coast. I shook my head.

"That place would be under too much machine-gun fire," I said. "Besides, sir, we've been practising cliff landing for eighteen months."

"All right, then," the Admiral agreed after further discussion, "but your men will have to swim the last bit."

"We've done it before and we can do it again," I said; but I was certain we could make a dry landing.

There was no point in arguing with the navy: their viewpoint was different from ours. They were used to a nice, tidy landing place, a beach or jetty; but they were most co-operative and could always be persuaded.

At this point the telephone rang on the Admiral's desk. The flagship at Scapa Flow is connected to the land telephone system. Tovey answered and for the next few minutes answered a rather long discourse from the other end in monosyllables. When he hung up he turned to me.

"That was the Prime Minister," he said. "What am I going to tell him if the Vaagso raid is a failure?"

"There will be no failure, sir," I promised. "We shall carry it off."

He seemed pleased with this assurance and raised no further obstacles to the plan.

I returned to London to complete the planning. One of my first acts was to see the Norwegians who were providing a party of a dozen men to come with us. Captain Martin Linge, who had accompanied me to the Lofotens earlier in the year, was in charge of the party. He had been most helpful before and I liked him personally. He smiled broadly when he saw me.

"I'm delighted that we meet again."

I returned the compliment. Then I noticed to my horror that his companions were talking quite openly of the coming raid, mentioning top-secret details and even the geographical place names of Vaagso and Maaloy.

"I hope no one else will be told these details," I said to Linge. "I'm satisfied with everything, except security."

"These fellows are all discreet," he assured me.

But he promised that no one else would be told. Still, I was worried about this matter and it kept returning to my mind to nag me. We were never frightened of ordinary opposition, but the thought of a slip in security and the consequent reception committee waiting for us on the beaches was not pleasant.

I arrived back in Largs two days before the unit was to leave for Scapa Flow. One of my men came to see me, a dark and restless soldier named Cross who was always mad keen to operate. Obviously distressed, he said:

"Sir, my wife has gone off with another man. I think if I can get down to see her, maybe I can put things right."

I had, of course, been unable to divulge to the soldiers that an operation was imminent. I granted Cross two days' leave, impressing on him that he must be back by then. Finding his domestic troubles more difficult to settle than he had thought, he overstayed his leave by one day. When he got back No. 3 Commando had left. Miserable over his personal problem and distraught at missing the raid, Cross deserted. He joined the Merchant Service in which he served with distinction for nearly a year, until the police picked him up and returned him to us. He was to come to my attention again at a later date.

H.M.S. *Prince Charles* and H.M.S. *Prince Leopold* arrived in the Clyde, and we embarked in mid-December, sailing immediately for Scapa Flow to carry out final rehearsals.

My basic plan was that Charles Haydon should be in overall command and direct things from H.M.S. *Kenya*; Jack Churchill would take a party to Maaloy Island, consisting of

COMMANDO

Nos. 5 and 6 Troops, and I should take Nos. 1, 2, 3 and 4
Troops to deal with the town of Vaagso. Charles Haydon
would have a floating reserve under his direction, for which
either of us could call. This floating reserve should consist of
two troops of No. 2 Commando.

The Royal Air Force was providing us with fighter cover for
the operation, and in addition was providing three Hampden
aeroplanes to come in very low and drop smoke bombs on the
beaches at the exact moment when the landing craft reached
the shore. I remember one of the Hampden pilots saying to
me during the London planning:

"I shall be roaring with laughter looking at you fellows
going in to land." Actually, at the moment in question, we
were doing most of the laughing, as his aircraft came in at
nought feet in a shower of tracer and very narrowly missed
hitting a steep cliff.

H.M.S. *Kenya* and four destroyers formed our immediate
naval support. All these ships were to bombard Maaloy
Island for ten minutes immediately prior to the landing.

Every single detail of the attack and of our equipment was
carefully worked out. As regards ammunition, it was decided that
each man should carry a hundred rounds, and that each Bren
gun was to have fifty magazines available, some of these to be
carried on the men and the rest placed in Commando Reserve
under the Administrative Officer. Twenty-five rounds of pistol
ammunition were to be carried by all officers armed with these
weapons; most officers also carried three or four spare Bren
magazines. Similarly, every detail of medical equipment was
worked out. Nursing orderlies were each to carry a surgical
haversack containing shell dressings, morphia, syringes, water
bottles and many other small medical items. The Medical
Officer himself carried two of these haversacks.

All the rehearsals went well, but we had very severe weather.
The evening trips to meetings in the flagship and elsewhere
were made in landing craft carried in our ex-Belgian ships.
The Commander of the landing craft flotilla carried in *Prince
Charles* was called Hastings; he was the son of Sir Patrick
Hastings and he was an expert at his job.

These expeditions were of a very hazardous nature, as the
navy had not forgotten the *Royal Oak* episode, and were quite

76

prepared to fire on any small craft approaching them out of the night. The nights were pitch black, and some of the coxswains of the landing craft had difficulty in finding their way round the anchorage, for which I did not blame them. I did more of these expeditions than anybody else, and in a few days was quite good at navigation within the limits of Scapa Flow.

Admiral Mountbatten visited us during the final rehearsal and spoke to the men.

"This is my first experience in telling people what to do in an action without going myself," he said, "and I don't like it. You needn't be too gentle with these Germans. When my ship the *Kelly* was sunk off Crete, the Luftwaffe machine-gunned us while we were swimming in the water. I regard you as my test pilots. Nobody knows quite what is going to happen and you are the ones who are going to find out. I have a great respect for test pilots."

We sailed from Scapa Flow on Christmas Eve. The first leg of our journey, to the Shetlands, was a rough one. Our cross-channel steamers were not designed for the battering given by these northern seas. Parts of our ship which should have remained solid came loose. The walls of my cabin, for instance, began to slide and make strange metallic noises. To prevent sickness, I took Joe Brunton's remedy of beer, cheese and pickled onions. It worked fine for me, but, although I passed it on to my brother officers, they seemed to find the cure more distasteful than the illness itself. I don't think any of us will remember this as our most cheerful Christmas. Yet discipline was in no way relaxed.

Every soldier was turned out on deck while we inspected the mess decks. The ship rolled to sixty degrees. We could hear our men singing the Vera Lynn favourite, "Yours." I had to admire their guts. These men were on their way to do battle; many were seasick; yet they sang.

When we arrived at Sollum Voe, in the Shetlands, an inspection revealed that everything forward in the ship was flooded to a depth of fourteen feet. Guard rails on the forecastle were smashed. The forward gun support was stove in and stores were flooded. The forward decks leaked and water was up to the doorsills of the sergeants' mess and elsewhere.

At four in the afternoon of Christmas Day the Hunt-class destroyer *Chiddingford* came alongside and helped pump 145 tons of water out of *Prince Charles*. We were seaworthy again.

As many other ships had sustained damage it was decided to wait a whole day in the Shetlands to complete the necessary repairs and to give everybody a night's sleep. The soldiers had had their Christmas dinner and were all fully recovered. All our officers were in great spirits. I had a drink with Algy Forrester and said to him:

"These Germans at Vaagso won't be so happy tomorrow night."

Algy said, very quietly, "I personally intend to see that there won't be any to be happy."

As night fell, on Boxing Day, the ships sailed again for Vaagso, Admiral Tovey covering our approach with the major units of the Atlantic Fleet, including his flagship, *King George V*. The submarine *Tuna* had preceded us and was lying off the entrance to Vaagsfjord to act as a navigational beacon on our way in. H.M.S. *Kenya* led our particular convoy, flying the flag of Admiral Burrough. She was followed by the destroyer H.M.S. *Chiddingford*; then came the *Charles* and *Leopold* carrying the troops with the destroyers *Onslow*, *Offa* and *Oribi* following close behind.

We were called at 4 a.m. I had often read in descriptions of naval battles that the sailors wore clean underclothes so as to minimise the risk of infection from wounds, so I put on a clean vest and pair of pants and told all the others to do the same. I took great trouble to check up on every item of my equipment. On this operation I carried a Colt .45 pistol with three spare magazines. All these magazines were discharged by the end of the day but I never again went into action carrying a pistol only, as these weapons do not give confidence when opposed to a man with a rifle. We had a good breakfast at 5 a.m. and carried with us a small compact haversack ration. In my case, and in nearly all other cases, this ration was untouched when we returned to the ship at 3 p.m. The excitement was too great to allow time off for eating.

Off Vaagsfjord at 7 a.m. we picked up the *Tuna* as planned. The surge of excitement which was running through our ship had erased all thought of seasickness. We entered the fjord, a spectacular passage between great, snow-covered hills. We were to land at first light, ten minutes to nine. The *Prince Charles* and *Prince Leopold* pulled into a small bay. The troops filed into the landing craft and these were lowered to the cold waters of the fjord. Then *Kenya*, two hundred yards behind us, opened the bombardment of Maaloy Island where the Germans manned a coast defence battery. We started the run-in in our landing craft.

About a hundred yards from our landing place, I fired ten red Very light signals. This told the ships to stop firing and the aircraft to come in with their smoke bombs. As I leaped from the leading landing craft three Hampden bombers passed over me at zero feet with a roar. As they did so they loosed their bombs, which seemed to flash and then mushroom like miniature atom explosions. Some of the phosphorus came back in a great flaming sheet. Next thing I knew both my sleeves were on fire. Fortunately I wore leather gloves and beat the flames out before they could eat through my four layers of clothing to the skin. The beaching had been made, dry, against snow-covered rocks which rose thirty or forty feet in an almost sheer wall. For the moment, we were unopposed and hidden from the enemy by smoke.

Unfortunately, however, one of the Hampdens was hit by anti-aircraft fire as she came in. Out of control, she dropped a bomb on an incoming landing craft. Bursting, the phosphorus inflicted terrible burns amongst the men. The craft, too, burst into flames. Grenades, explosives, and small arms ammunition were detonated in a mad mixture of battle noises. We pushed the emptied craft out to sea where it could do us no harm, and Sam Corry, our big, efficiently calm Irish doctor, taking charge of the casualties, sent them back to the *Prince Charles*. The rest of us turned to the battle.

Vaagso is built on one narrow street, three-quarters of a mile long, which runs parallel to, and about fifty yards from, the fjord. Behind the street, which was lined with unpainted wooden buildings, nearly sheer rocks rose to several hundred feet. I heard Johnny Giles yell, "Come on," and saw him disappear with his No. 3 Troop into the smoke.

That was the last I saw of Johnny. Fifteen minutes later he

79

was dead, killed in an assault on the back of a house. He and his men had shot three Germans who had been firing on them from the house, then rushed it. They went through the rooms and as Johnny entered the last room a fourth German jumped in front of him and shot him.

At about the time Johnny met his death I went into a large oil factory near our landing beach. I was looking for Johann Gotteberg, who had been named to us as the chairman of the local quislings and was the owner of this factory. Meanwhile Bill Bradley prepared the factory for demolition. I saw a middle-aged man who seemed to be attending the machinery with extraordinary concentration, considering the circumstances.

"Who is that man?" I asked my Norwegian guide, a native of Vaagso.

"That is Gotteberg, the owner."

I had him arrested. A few minutes later he had a first-class view of his factory being blown up.

Algy Forrester went off like a rocket with his No. 4 Troop down the street of the town, leaving a trail of dead Germans behind him. The troop had just lost Arthur Komrower, who had suffered severe leg and back injuries when he was pinned between a landing craft and a rock. The third officer of 4 Troop was Bill Lloyd, who, with Algy, had developed the technique of landing on rough and rocky shores. Bill hardly got going before he was shot, clean through the neck. That was the end of him for this operation.

Algy waded in, shouting and cheering his men, throwing grenades into each house as they came to it and firing from the hip with his tommy gun. He looked wild and dangerous. I shouldn't have liked to have been a German in his path. He had absolutely no fear. He led an assault against the German headquarters, in the Ulvasund Hotel, and was about to toss a grenade in when one of the enemy, firing through the front door, shot him. As he fell he landed on his own grenade, which exploded a second later. This rough landing at Vaagso was the first time we had put into operational practice the system he and Bill Lloyd had developed. For Algy it was also the last.

Other casualties in Algy's troop were heavy. Captain Martin Linge, my Norwegian friend, had also been attached to No. 4. When the attack was briefly held up after Algy's death, he kept things moving, but only for a few minutes. He was killed in exactly the same way as Forrester, shot as he tried to force open a door. I had spoken to Martin just as he left the beach.

"This is good, Colonel," he had said, laughing. "We'll have a party at the Mayfair to celebrate when we get back."

He was a very gallant and fearless ally and would have made an ideal Commando soldier.

The Germans had a tank in a garage near the Ulvesund Hotel, about 150 yards up the street, a fact of which we were aware through our intelligence. The tank was an old one, but if it were brought out on to the street it could wreak havoc amongst us with its gun. After Martin Linge's death, Sergeant Cork and Johnnie Dowling of 1 Troop managed to reach the tank, still in the garage, and blow it up. Unfortunately Cork used too heavy a charge and didn't get away quickly enough. He was caught in the explosion and died of wounds. Johnnie was untouched. Corporal "Knocker" White was left in command of Forrester's troop. He performed the job so gallantly that he was to earn a Distinguished Conduct Medal for it.

From our out-of-doors, snow-covered headquarters near the landing place, I could see everything that took place on Maaloy. Nos. 5 and 6 Troops, only fifty yards from the beach when the naval barrage lifted, were up the slopes of the island like a flash. I saw them advancing through the smoke in perfect extended order. Jack Churchill, who had played them in with his bagpipes, was leading them with considerable dash. On landing, Peter Young saw a German running back to man his gun position. "I was able to shoot him," Peter told me later. Ten minutes after this, Young reached the company office on Maaloy. One of the German company clerks made the literally fatal mistake of trying to wrest Peter's rifle from him. Small pockets of resistance were quickly cleaned up and many prisoners were taken, including two Norwegian women of easy virtue who had been consoling the German soldiers.

The fighting in the town was still hot and heavy, however, and I had Charlie Head, my Signals Officer for this raid, send a message to the headquarters ship asking for the floating reserve, and another to Jack Churchill on Maaloy asking if he, too, could help. Jack promptly sent 6 Troop under Peter Young; and Charles Haydon ordered the floating reserve to the far end of Vaagso. We were now attacking on two fronts.

Back in the main street, where our attack had been stalled, Peter Young with 6 Troop got things moving again. I left the Adjutant to control our headquarters and joined him. It was very noisy: there were the different sounds from the various calibres of small arms; artillery exchanges between *Kenya* and a coast defence battery somewhere down the fjord; anti-aircraft fire from the ships against the attacking Messerschmitts; the demolitions; and the crackling roar of flames. I heard one signaller complaining how difficult it was to receive messages.

"This is bloody awful! A man can hardly hear himself think!"

Our opposition was much stiffer than I had expected. It was not until later that I learned that about fifty men from an exceptionally good German unit were spending Christmas leave at Vaagso.

As I tried to catch up with Peter Young I saw him and George Herbert throwing grenades through windows and doors. They appeared to be enjoying themselves. I finally joined them in a timber yard which had only one entrance off the main street. Part of our plan had been to dump many sacks of grenades near the landing place. Our Administrative Officer had organised a gang of loyal Norwegian civilians who followed close behind the leading troops, carrying these sacks, and offering the troops replenishments of grenades as often as they were needed.

Suddenly, in a strange interval when artillery and demolitions seemed to pause for their second wind, there was an eerie, unexpected stillness. Half of No. 6 Troop were clustered in the timber yard. A single rifle shot rang out and a man fell dead beside me. I thought the shot had come from a house, about twenty yards away, on the other side of the small yard. We all started firing furiously at the windows of the house. I emptied my revolver, feeling strangely helpless, for there was only one exit to the yard and unless we did something quickly it seemed certain the sniper would pick us all off, one by one.

Another shot came from the house and another man fell dead. I think this was the first time in warfare that I truly felt fear. I didn't like it.

We crouched behind a pile of timber. The sniper fired whenever one of us moved. Soon he picked off a third of our number. He was shooting right down at us from a first floor window.

There was a shed just behind our cover and George Herbert disappeared into it. "Captain Young," he called, "I've found a tin of petrol!"

"Put some in a bucket, Sergeant," Peter called back. "When you've done that we'll all stand up and give you covering fire while you toss it into the house."

Herbert obeyed, and the others followed the petrol up by lobbing grenades through the windows. There was a great burst of flame. Very soon the wooden house was burned to the ground, a funeral pyre for the sniper. I wasn't sorry to leave that timber yard.

It was just about then that Lieutenant Denis O'Flaherty was wounded. He had been leading assault after assault on enemy-held houses and was leading an attack on the steamship wharf when a sniper, concealed in a warehouse, hit him in the eye. The bullet came out through his throat. O'Flaherty, a brave soldier, had been wounded twice before. This most serious wound was to cost him eight major operations and two years in hospital. He lost his eye but never his spirit. Later, still fighting for Britain, he was decorated by the Americans for gallantry in Korea.

After the affair of the timber yard, when the attack got moving down the main street again, a door on the fjord side of the street suddenly opened and a German lobbed out a grenade. It rolled between my feet and stopped. I was standing on a corner and instinctively took a tremendous dive for shelter round the edge of the building. I landed on my face, just in time to hear the grenade go off. I escaped with a couple of small bits of the grenade in my palm, but my orderly was badly wounded.

About thirty seconds later, the same door opened and the German who had tossed the grenade came out with his hands up and expressing his earnest desire to surrender. I was prepared to accept this, but one of my men thought otherwise. He advanced on the German. "Nein! Nein!" the German yelled, a small man, yellow and scared.

Our man was so angry that he shot the German dead, through the stomach. This, of course, is one of the tricky problems in warfare. Can a man throw a death-dealing grenade one second and surrender the next? I hardly think he can expect much mercy.

Then I saw Bob Clement organising an attack on another building farther down the street. With Lance-Sergeant Culling, he led the way. As they approached the front door, a German threw a percussion grenade at Culling's face, killing him instantly. Clement kept a brisk fire going into the building and called for Sergeant Ramsey and the mortar detachment, posting men all around to prevent any German from escaping. Ramsey got a direct hit on the roof with his third round and them pumped several dozen mortar bombs through the hole. The place was soon blazing. On my way back, when the flames had died down, I counted twelve German corpses inside.

This incident was to end the most severe phase of the fighting. We were now well on top, and I felt sure we would achieve every objective of the raid. I remember marvelling at the courage of the newsreel and press photographers, who never roamed far from the leading soldiers. Harry Regnold, the army movie cameraman, Jack Ramsden of Movietone News and E. G. Mallandine, an army stills photographer (now with *Illustrated* magazine) were continually in the forefront of the battle.

All this time there had been a good deal of air activity. The R.A.F. fighter cover consisted of Blenheims, which, although no match for the Messerschmitts, nevertheless put up a gallant performance. It was a heartrending sight to see two or three of the Blenheims shot down by the Messerschmitts, which were able to out-manœuvre their slower and heavier opponents. However, they were successful in their main objective of keeping the enemy bombers away from the ships.

When we got to the end of the street, I looked at my watch. It was 1.45 p.m. I was astonished to realise that I had been away from my headquarters for two hours. It was nearly time to make our withdrawal. I called a troop commanders' meeting to issue final orders.

"We'll not be going any further," I said. "We'll withdraw a troop at a time. No. 2 troop with Clement will go first; then No. 6 with Young; and No. 1 with Bradley will cover, coming last."

On the way back down the main street, I found many houses were now burning fiercely. Pieces of burning wood fell on the road. I was wryly amused to notice that many of my men, who had been entirely without fear in battle, were now scared to death by the flames. I took the lead.

"Come on with me! You won't get hurt!"

And I ran quickly through the avenue of fire. When we were nearly back to headquarters I saw a handsome young German lying the gutter, seriously wounded in the chest and obviously near death. He smiled at me. When he beckoned, I walked over and spoke to him. He could speak no English, but indicated that he wished to shake hands. We did. I think what he meant, and I agreed, was that it had been a good, clean battle.

While the street fighting had been going on, the destroyers *Oribi* and *Onslow* had not been idle. They had set about destroying enemy shipping in the anchorage. The original intention was to bring the larger ships back to England; but the Germans were too quick at scuttling to make this possible. Nevertheless, it was some satisfaction to see ship after ship settling to the bottom. *Onslow* and *Oribi* often had to administer the *coup de grâce*. Boarding parties, moving quickly, were able to recover valuable documents. Ten ships, totalling eighteen thousand tons, were sent to the bottom.

During the fighting Charlie was flashing messages from our beach headquarters through to Brigadier Haydon. When Charlie was not up to the latest fighting progress he did the best he could to reassure the Brigadier. "Everything going well," "progress satisfactory," were the phrases he used again and again when, for all he knew, we might all have been massacred.

"I couldn't see any point in interrupting you at your work," he said to me later.

At the peak period of the battle Charlie was passing signals at the rate of forty an hour.

Snipers made the evacuation of the wounded a considerable problem, but Sam Corry and his medical orderlies did a wonderful job. Sam was a man with a great fighting heart. He could not resist the temptation to take part in the battle. I saw him several times, first attending to his wounded, then seizing their rifles to get a few shots at the enemy. Handcarts were used as far as possible to transport the wounded to Sam Corry's regimental aid post, just off the beach. From this point they had to be carried on stretchers down the almost sheer rocks leading to the boats.

We carried out demolitions so effectively that we used most of the stores we brought ashore for this purpose, 300 lbs. of plastic explosive, 1,100 lbs. of guncotton, 150 lbs. of ammonal explosive, 150 incendiary bombs, sixty guncotton primers and 1,400 feet of fuse. Before any German-occupied building was blown up, a member of our intelligence section searched through it for documents. This precaution paid off beautifully when we found the master code for the whole of the German navy. For many weeks to come, as a result of this priceless discovery, the Admiralty in London was able freely to decipher all German naval signal messages. This, of course, helped us greatly in the conduct of the war at sea.

The withdrawal and re-embarkation was now going smoothly and silently. Charlie Head and I were the last two on the beach, and I could see that he wanted to be the last man off.

"Go on, get in!" I said, in a tone which indicated that this was an order, not a request.

He grinned and obeyed, thus giving me, beyond dispute, the honour of being first in, last out, on this operation which was to be described in *The Times* a day or two later as "the perfect raid."

The two Norwegian tarts found on Maaloy were taken with other prisoners on board the *Prince Charles*. Laughing as if it were a great joke, I think they hoped to carry on their business without interruption, despite the changed fortunes of war. They were put in the doctor's cabin; he was so busy attending the wounded that there was no chance of his needing it.

They were quick to replace their battle-stained clothes by helping themselves to two pairs of the doctor's best pyjamas, and wore them with necklines which plunged far below the demands of decency. I am glad to say their sentries ignored them.

Despite all the events of the day, the news had not reached every German-held port, and as we pulled out a large German merchant ship was coming in. The *Prince Charles* joined in the bombardment, but I fear her fire was inaccurate. The ship was soon sunk by H.M.S. *Kenya*.

I went up to the bridge and saw her Captain, and he said that I had a very warlike appearance as blood from my hand had spread to a good many portions of my clothing, my tunic had a large burn in it, my pistol was still in my hand, and three grenades were lying on top of the Mae West inside the tunic. The Mae West, blown up hard, makes a very convenient lodging place for things of this kind.

We pulled out to sea at a good speed and the resourceful Charlie Head soon conjured up a bottle of whisky. The day was not quite done. Before leaving Scapa Flow we had all been taught a few phrases of Norwegian and Charlie had added one of his own. Just before going to bed I took a walk round the boat deck and saw a lovely Norwegian girl who had embarked with us to go back to England. We got talking, and I could not resist the temptation to try out Charlie's phrase, "Yi ilsaka di," which means "I love you." To my surprise she understood despite my curious accent, and replied in English, "Me too." However, this promising episode soon came to an end as some sentry or other interfering person arrived on the scene.

Back at Scapa Flow, we had a most enthusiastic welcome from the Royal Navy, who until then had held the army in rather low esteem since they had been continually called upon to rescue and evacuate it. Things were different now. The *Kenya* sent a message that her ship's company thought our men were terrific. Admiral Burrough contributed several bottles of champagne towards a toast containing the same sentiments. Our success was acclaimed by Combined Operations

Headquarters and even our old enemies at the War Office applauded.

The operation could chalk up facts and figures on the balance sheet which made pleasant reading to me. Valuable German documents and codes had been taken. We had killed 120 of the enemy and brought back ninety-eight prisoners; this was the first reasonably large collection of German prisoners to be taken to Britain in the war. We had destroyed all enemy offices, many cars and lorries, the tank (a fifteen-tonner), five guns, petrol tanks, ammunition stores, barracks and telephone exchanges, beach mines, searchlights, lighthouses, W/T installations, and four factories.

By contrast, our casualties were reasonably light. Two ratings killed and two officers and four ratings wounded was the naval toll. Two officers and fifteen other ranks killed and five officers and forty-eight other ranks wounded was the military total. The Norwegian party lost one officer, Captain Linge, and two men had been wounded. Eight of our aircraft were missing.

I felt that at last No. 3 Commando had proved its worth as a raiding unit. The battle of Vaagso had been won against first-class opposition by the utter ruthlessness and complete professional competence of our officers and men. They stopped for nothing. Each house had to be taken and we had to destroy the people in it. Our attack had to be fast and deadly; we had a lot to do and a short time to do it. If one Commando soldier was shot down, his comrades always came forward to press the fighting on, throwing grenades, firing rifles and Bren guns. Never at any time was the impetus of the attack allowed to die down. Before Vaagso, late in 1941, the Germans had taken no real beating on land. Now, I felt, all our arduous training and my merciless rejection of the unsuitable and the unfit had been justified.

After our return, I spoke to all ranks.

"Future operations," I said, "must be regarded as the highlights of our lives. A very few of you didn't like the Vaagso operation and must leave the unit forthwith. Your behaviour and turn-out must be irreproachable at all times. Have all the fun that's going: drink, gambling, chasing the

girls, and so on, if it appeals to you; but if these things inter-
fere with your work they must be put aside. Personally, I
have long, quiet periods without any of these diversions and
recommend you to do the same. You must always behave
and look like super soldiers. If you cannot, then there is no
place for you in No. 3 Commando."

On New Year's Day, 1942, we had another wonderful
reception at Largs. In my mail was an unexpected Mention
in Despatches for the Lofoten raid which now seemed an
event of the dim past. We had a party that night. I know
there were many who whispered that they thought me callous
about our casualties at Vaagso. Nothing could be less true, a
fact which can be confirmed by the kind lady who brought
me a cup of tea at about five o'clock that New Year's afternoon. I had been thinking of my friends who had died in
that long, snowy street; and I was not ashamed to have her
find me in great distress. These gallant dead would not be
with us for the battles to come. Without them, we should
not have done so well at Vaagso.

Chapter VII

DIEPPE

TO REPLACE the killed, the wounded, and those who did not measure up in battle to the stiff requirements of the unit, No. 3 Commando had about eighty vacancies to fill after Vaagso. My recruiting methods at this time were irregular but effective. I simply gave my officers extra leave on condition that they returned with some suitable recruits. They would fulfil their end of the bargain by approaching commanding officers of other, non-Commando, units and calling for volunteers. Sometimes they got sent angrily away.

"But, dammit, you're after my best men!" the C.O. would roar.

Sometimes they were able to talk the C.O. round. At any rate, it did not take over-long to fill our ranks.

After a period of leave early in January, 1942, we took a very strong pull on ourselves, and got down to even tougher training than before. Everybody realised that Vaagso was merely a prelude to further severe operations. This training continued through the spring and early summer, and our new men settled down well. Several times operations were planned and postponed.

For some months, late in 1941, there had been discussions about a suitable headdress for the Commandos, and, after some research in the appropriate places, it was decided to adopt the green beret, green having an heraldic association with hunting. We had in mind Mr. Churchill's instructions that Commando troops were to be of the hunter class. A large order was placed for these green berets. At first it was considered that the steel helmet should still be worn in action, but No. 3 Commando always wore the green beret. I was sometimes criticised for this, the critics saying that we were risking head wounds, but the added activity given by a light headdress was worthwhile, and certainly in my own case,

90

mental as well as physical activity was hampered by wearing a steel helmet.

By this time our reputation was well established and we had many important visitors who came to see our training. Much of this training was passed on to the field army. Among these visitors, early in 1942, was General Alexander (now Lord Alexander, Minister of Defence). As we were walking round, the General left me for a moment and engaged Charlie Head in conversation. Charlie had just taken over as Adjutant and General Alexander was interested in the problem of cutting down office work.

"How many hours' work a day do you do in your office?" I heard him say to Charlie.

"About eight," Charlie replied, obviously trying to please.

General Alexander looked at him blankly.

"What the hell do you do for eight hours?"

Charlie, with his usual commonsense, saw at once that he was on the wrong track.

"Well," he admitted, "I spend about two hours in the office and the rest of the time helping with the training."

Early in July I was sent for from London where I saw Brigadier Laycock, who had taken over from Haydon.

"John, there's a big operation on against Dieppe," Laycock said. "We're going to use No. 3 Commando on the east flank and No. 4 on the west flank."

I was delighted and said so.

"There's a very practical reason for choosing you for the east," he continued. "You may have to climb some pretty steep cliffs and you've had the training for it."

Our task, he told me, would be to destroy or put out of action a large coast defence battery which commanded the entire anchorage off Dieppe. Of course the plan for the Dieppe raid was that the 2nd Canadian Division should attack the town frontally. No. 4 Commando was detailed to take a battery west of the town.

The battery which No. 3 Commando was to attack was sited near Berneval Le Grand, a small village half a mile from the sea. It was known as the Goebbels Battery. Before it were sheer cliffs rising three hundred feet from the Channel's shore, quite unclimbable. There were, however, two gullies half a mile apart which were possible avenues to the clifftops. Continual air reconnaissances were flown by the R.A.F. which revealed that the German defences were being intensified every day.

Bob Laycock said to me:

"You can see that it will be absolutely impossible for the ships to lie off Dieppe while your battery is in action. Can you guarantee to do the job?"

"Given a proper landing," I said, "you can be quite sure that our battery won't fire on the shipping."

Originally, airborne troops had been allotted the task of capturing these flank batteries, but it was thought that having two airborne operations going, in addition to the complicated major attack on Dieppe, would make things too difficult. Also, the airborne troops would, of course, have to be taken off by sea, so it was obviously much easier to use seaborne Commandos.

A further object of the raid was to bring on a major air battle with the Luftwaffe. The R.A.F. had, during the summer of 1942, started a series of fighter sweeps over northern France, but had found that it was very hard to bring the Luftwaffe to battle. It was rightly thought that if a landing was effected and a large concentration of shipping was lying off Dieppe, the German airmen would at last be forced to come in on a large scale. Seaford was to be our base as it had a good training area and was handy for embarkation at Newhaven. I got down to studying the air photographs, and a good many photographs of the beaches in a peaceful state, taken by pre-war holiday-makers.

I had taken a course in the interpretation of air photographs, so was able to do my own reading of the results of the gallant efforts of the airmen. I kept a lot of the information to myself, as it is not good for morale to see the continual build-up of probable opposition. I told our officers just enough to enable them to make their plans, using the cover plan of saying that the Cherbourg peninsula project had been revived; this project had come up early in the spring but had been abandoned. The intelligence summary told us that up to 350 troops were situated in the Berneval area, so it was evident that we had quite a battle on hand. I spotted what appeared to me to be

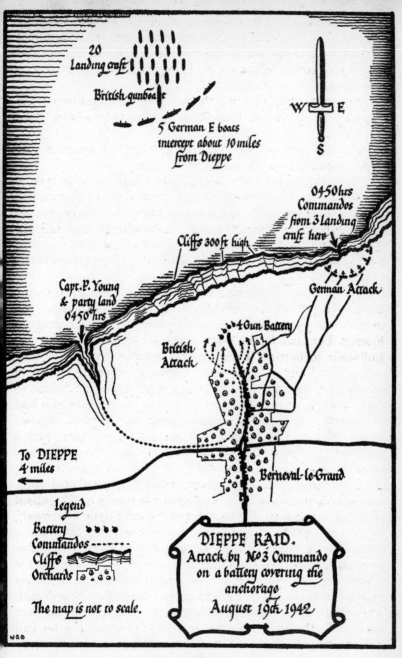

20
landing craft

British gunboat

5 German E boats
intercept about 10 miles
from Dieppe

W E
S

Cliffs 300 ft high

0450 hrs
Commandos
from 3 landing
craft here

Capt. P. Young
& party land
0450 hrs

German Attack

4 Gun Battery

British
Attack

To DIEPPE
4 miles

Berneval-le-Grand

Legend
Battery   ● ● ● ●
Commandos - - - - - -
Cliffs
Orchards

The map is not to scale.

DIEPPE RAID.
Attack by Nº 3 Commando
on a battery covering the
anchorage
August 19th 1942

W.R.D

93

"That's the way it goes, honey,
That's the way it goes."

Lieut. George Herbert, D.C.M., M.M.
T.S.M. "Lofty" King, M.M.

C.S.M. J. Dowling, M.M.
L/Cpl. Charlesworth.

:eut. (later Major) Charles Head, M.C.

Colonel (later Brigadier) Peter Young, D.S.O., M.C.

Admiral of the Fleet Lord Keyes talking to the Author after the Lofoten raid.

Our trail of destruction.
Landing craft leaving the Lofoten Islands.

Demolition squads at work in the Lofoten Islands.
"Flames curled over our heads in an alarming way."

H.M. King George VI talking to Algy Forrester.

Landing craft being lowered from the *Prince Charles*.
Scaling a cliff face.

"Many houses were now burning fiercely."
Denis O'Flaherty after being wounded at Vaagso.

"On your way, fella." (Stage 1.)
"On your way, fella." (Stage 2.)

Jack Churchill inspecting a gun captured on Maaloy Island.
A burning oil factory at Vaagso.

No. 3 Commando Bridge.
General Montgomery visiting us at Termoli.

The Author leaving Buckingham Palace with his wife and daughter
after being awarded the D.S.O.

Watching for snipers in Osnabruck.
Wesel: on guard against German rearguards.

"The party took place three hundred yards from the front line."
Brigadier B. W. Leicester, the Author, and Brigadier D. Mills-Roberts.

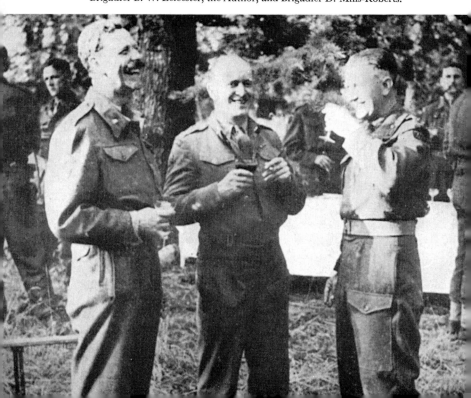

Meeting No. 3 Commando at Tilbury, 1945.
No. 3 Commando leaving Tilbury.

Disbandment, Victoria Station.
Afterwards: Charlie Head, the Author, and John Charles Head.

definite machine-gun positions at either end of the beach, opposite the more easterly of the two gullies, and could also see that there were thick belts of wire in the entrance to both gullies. Nevertheless, I was entirely confident that our battle-trained officers and men would overcome all these obstacles. The photographs showed that the beach was rocky and rough. This did not affect our landing, which was timed for high water, but re-embarkation, four hours later when the tide had dropped, was going to be difficult.

One or two of the more clever boys soon spotted the dissimilarity in the cliff formations between Cherbourg and Dieppe from studying the photographs, but on the whole security was well kept.

"You needn't pull my leg, John," Charlie Head said to me one day. "I know where we're going, or pretty close. How about Newhaven-Dieppe?"

I said nothing for a moment. Then:

"If you think that, you needn't tell anybody else."

I saw by the photographs that the two gullies gave us excellent cover, and the needed approaches inland. Our plan was to make landings of about equal strength on each beach. The two parties were to work their way inland, coming in a co-ordinated attack upon the battery through the village of Berneval. If one landing failed, the other should be able to neutralise the battery by keeping it under fire, so that it could not harm our shipping.

Our channel crossing from Newhaven was to be made in twenty small, American-designed landing craft, with Commando headquarters in a steam gunboat. Recalling our unfortunate Guernsey experience, I was not happy about the prospect of a sixty-seven-mile passage in small boats.

Peter Young, now my second-in-command, was to take charge of the more westerly landing. I was to force the entrance to the eastern gulley.

Given a proper landing, I was absolutely satisfied that we should be able to do our job, but just in case an undue number of the small landing craft should break down, I put a note in our orders saying that if the capture and destruction of the battery proved an impossible or lengthy task, owing to a proportion of the Commandos not arriving on the beaches, the guns should be engaged by fire at the earliest possible moment, and should be continually harassed by snipers.

I telephoned to Peter Young at Largs and told him to get the Commando down at once to Seaford so that they should be on the spot for final training. No. 3 Commando had a tremendous send-off from the townspeople at Largs.

From time to time one or another of my officers went with me to London to study photographs and maps at Combined Operations Headquarters in Whitehall. This meant, of course, that a few others in addition to myself knew of our destination. One morning, coming back to the unit's new temporary headquarters in Seaford, the young officer accompanying me fell asleep in the electric train. He awoke suddenly, during that period of almost total silence when an electric train stops. In what seemed to me to be a terribly loud voice, he remarked,

"I wonder if this Dieppe business will come off."

Horrified, I took a quick walk down the corridor to see if anyone could have overheard him. The coach was empty except for a naval officer. I happened to know he was going on the operation, and had been briefed about it. Soon after getting back to my headquarters an MI5 man called on me.

"A dreadful thing has happened," he said to me. "Two of your officers were heard using the word 'Dieppe' in the train this morning."

"That *is* a grave matter," I agreed. "I can assure you that I'll make the most searching enquiries."

He gave me a hard look and left. That was the last I heard of the affair; I reprimanded the officer but did not dismiss him. I believe I was justified in my action. He proved himself, not only at Dieppe but in the years to come, to be a first-class Commando soldier, discreet and devoted to duty.

Seaford was most invigorating as frequent visits from low-flying German aircraft gave us the necessary warlike atmosphere, which had been lacking in the west of Scotland. Rehearsals and planning started on an intensive scale, and I have never been more confident. We had superb officers and men, perfectly trained and with battle experience.

The standard of our officers at this time was very high; in

fact such performers as Bill Lloyd and John Pooley could
not be fitted into Captains' vacancies. I consulted our Brigade
Headquarters and found that several other Commandos would
be delighted to have them as Captains; I told Bill Lloyd and
Pooley of this, but, after thinking things over, they decided
to forgo the promotion and remain with No. 3 Commando.
Bill Lloyd had made a miraculous recovery from his wound
at Vaagso. The bullet had passed clean through his neck
without touching any vital spot. Neither he nor John Pooley
wished to miss the forthcoming operation.

Every portion of the operation on land was rehearsed a
dozen times on the hills to the west of the village of Alfriston,
situated a few miles from Seaford, and I then got into touch
with Commander Wyburg, our immediate naval commander,
and arranged a full-scale rehearsal with landing craft. Owing
to German air activity we had to conduct this rehearsal in
the sheltered waters of the Solent, as it was obviously impossible
to take a trip out into mid-Channel. I arranged for a special
train to Portsmouth, and the Commando embarked at 8 p.m.
on a Sunday evening late in July. In order to reproduce as
nearly as possible the sixty-seven-mile crossing to Dieppe, the
craft circled in formation all night off the Isle of Wight. This
gave the naval personnel a great chance of trying out their
formations and got our soldiers used to spending many hours
in the cramped conditions of the landing craft. On this
rehearsal, only one landing craft broke down, and the two
landings were duly made on the Isle of Wight at first light.
As a result of this trial, Wyburg and I told Admiral Mountbatten that, given fairly calm weather and a strong escort,
the Bernaval landings would be accomplished.

On the whole, equipment carried was much the same as
that for the Vaagso raid, except in the matter of the demolition
stores. There was no need for the enormous amount of explosive needed to blow up the Vaagso factories. All we needed
were a number of special charges suitable for blowing up the
guns and the ammunition store. John Pooley was at this time
our Demolitions Officer, and he distributed his charges over
many different boat loads. Thus any fair-sized party of our
troops arriving at the battery would have sufficient demolition
charges to blow up the guns.

On this operation we decided to increase the proportion of tracer ammunition carried. This was partly to increase accuracy of fire, and partly because of the great moral effect tracer gives by day and by night. When you can see the bullets coming at you it is far worse than merely hearing the report. On every operation till the end of the war we continued this policy, sometimes adding incendiary and armour-piercing bullets as well.

One of our office staff chose this moment to absent himself with a considerable sum of money. I told Captain Martin, our Administrative Officer, to go after him, and told Charlie Head to render the necessary assistance. Charlie, always the man of direct action, rang up Superintendent Nat Thorp, one of the big five at Scotland Yard, whom we both knew well, and told him our troubles. A few hours later Nat rang through to say that he had picked up the man in question, only a few pounds being missed. During our years together, quite a few people apart from the Germans, found that taking on the old firm of Head and Slater was a formidable proposition.

It was beautiful hot weather, and a daily diversion in our office was the arrival of the lovely Miss Maxine Birley, now Comtesse de la Falaise, frequently referred to as the best dressed woman in Paris. She was very kindly trying to organise a dance for us at her father's lovely house nearby, but her arrival in beachwear caused all work to stop in the office and it was always about half an hour after this visit before I could get any sense out of the office staff. My office was upstairs, so I was able to take a detached, though not disinterested, view of these proceedings. It was a very tricky problem as, according to our invariable rule before an operation, we were all but teetotal, and no dance or similar celebration was allowed. I think this clever and beautiful lady must have sensed what was going on as she stopped her visits but duly organised a splendid dance on the night after Dieppe.

Seaford was full of Canadians who were at first not friendly with our soldiers. In these wartime conditions attractive girls were in short supply, and when our men started taking out some of the girls, previously friendly with the Canadians, trouble became inevitable. A trooper named Joe Court, a fine Commando soldier and athlete, and one of our sergeants went out one night with two Wrens whom they knew well. The party went into a café full of Canadians. A large Canadian walked over, looked at Joe Court and said:

"Commandos, we —— them."

Joe very calmly put down his teacup and said:

"You do, do you?" and then unloosed a terrific blow, knocking the Canadian unconscious.

The other Canadians in the café respected the fact that Joe was able to look after himself, his sergeant and their girl friends, and from that day there was no more trouble. A great friendship sprang up between No. 3 Commando and the Canadians, which lasted until the end of the war.

Towards the end of July, I was called to a meeting at Combined Operations Headquarters to help draft the final operation order for the raid and to clear up remaining problems. The meeting was presided over by Admiral Mountbatten and was attended, amongst others, by the late Air Marshal Leigh-Mallory, representing the R.A.F., Captain Hughes-Hallett, for the navy, and General Roberts, commanding the Canadian Division.

It was customary at these meetings for everyone to put up his point of view and then for the presiding officer to weigh the pros and cons and make his decisions. Leigh-Mallory was pessimistic about the raid.

"I don't like this," he said. "I don't think there's enough preparation in the way of heavy bombing. I think these Canadians are going to have a bad time in the centre."

I agreed with him. After our recent tough battle at Vaagso, against comparatively minor defences, I was most doubtful of the Canadians' success at Dieppe which was heavily defended. But it wasn't my place to say so. I was there only to comment on the role of No. 3 Commando out on the flank. General Roberts did almost no talking, although it was up to him to speak if the plans were not exactly to his liking. He, like the rest of us, had every opportunity to speak up. Unlike Leigh-Mallory, he made no adverse comment at all.

The security question was discussed for a long time. It

was decided that the security of the units taking part was good, and that the most likely source of leakages would be from the large number of staff officers who wished to come on the operation as spectators, with an admirable desire to learn the trade of combined operations from personal observation. It was decided to concentrate all these spectators in the West Country several days before the raid; they were to be told that an operation was imminent in the Atlantic Islands. They were then to be brought to the embarkation ports at the very last moment.

Admiral Mountbatten asked Lord Lovat, commanding No. 4 Commando, and me whether we would be willing to take on the raid a party from the 1st United States Rangers, twenty officers and men. The American Rangers were the equivalent of our Commandos, and had gone through a rigorous training at our Commando depot in Scotland. We were both glad to accept them. In fact, for my part, I was thrilled at the thought of commanding the first American land forces to operate in Europe in this war. They wanted battle experience: they were to get it.

The American party duly arrived at Seaford with Captain Roy Murray in command. He was small, dark and cheerful, overflowing with eagerness to co-operate. I admired the American weapons, especially the Garand which I handled for the first time.

"Would you like to try one on the range?" Murray asked.

"Very much."

I did try it.

"This is exactly the weapon we've been looking for," I told him. Murray was delighted.

"We've got a few to spare," he said. "Would you like to keep that one for yourself, Colonel?"

I could hardly express my pleasure. Murray gave one to Peter Young as well, and distributed a few to others of my troop commanders. I found the weapon accurate, easy to handle, quick, and generous with fire power: much better than the short-range tommy gun I had been using. Without a doubt, the Garand was a big advance on any rifle we had yet handled in the Commandos.

I spoke to the Rangers as a party when they arrived and told them that for the period of the operation they would be an integral part of No. 3 Commando. I explained our system of instantly returning to his unit any man found unsuitable. All the Americans gladly accepted this and they were ready to work hard, play hard and accept our fairly tough way of life. I divided them up among our troops and we found them comfortable billets. Everybody liked them and enjoyed their company.

My own billet at Seaford was at a pleasant house on top of a hill at the back of the town. One night I had just gone to bed when I heard curious noises in the hall. The lady who owned the house was away, and only her servant was there. I put on my slippers and went down in pyjamas to find an enormous Canadian walking round the hall. He had broken in through a small window. Fortunately, he was extremely drunk, so I spoke to him nicely, and gave him a little push into a comfortable armchair, where he slept most amiably. I started to telephone the police and most unwisely ended my message with the words, "I will detain him until you come." This brought the Canadian to life in a big way, and he jumped to his feet shouting:

"Detain me nothing! Say, I could knock hell out of you."

Mentally I quite agreed with him, as I did not feel my best in pyjamas in the middle of the night, and faced with an angry man six inches taller than myself. I measured him for a blow strictly forbidden in the Queensbury Rules, but suddenly he again became amiable and another gentle push put him back in the comfortable armchair, where he slept heavily, and in the end went off in a good humour with a small and rather elderly special constable.

Cross, the man who had unwillingly deserted before Vaagso, was brought in under arrest at this time. Charlie Head arranged for a quick court martial. I was Cross's principal witness. I spoke so freely in his favour that the court granted a discharge on my private undertaking that Cross would be in the thick of the coming battle. After the court martial, Cross came to me.

"Thank you, Colonel," he said. "You can rely on me to do my stuff."

"You keep your word and I'll look after you," I said.

It was mid-August and everything was ready.

Peter Young and I visited the Canadian Divisional Headquarters, as they wished to hear of our Vaagso experiences. We told them all we could. They were full of confidence, but I was afraid they were in for a very tough time, owing to the strength of the defences on the beaches they were due to attack.

Our landing craft had arrived at Newhaven and were concealed under an enormous canvas screen. The German air force was obviously suspicious and flew at least twelve sorties a day, taking photographs of the large concentration of shipping assembled at Newhaven.

Anthony Head, now Secretary of State for War, and not related to Charlie, was, in the summer of 1942, a Staff Officer at Combined Operations Headquarters. He arranged to ring me up and tell me to collect some stores on a certain date. The date mentioned was to be that of the raid and this was to be a signal for me to get my unit cracking. One day the phone rang.

"You'd better collect those stores on the morning of August 19th," Anthony Head said.

I thanked him pleasantly.

I called the troops in from their billets to brief them. They had instructions to bring all their equipment as I could allow no one to have outside contact once place names had been mentioned. I briefed the soldiers personally, leaving it to the troop commanders to fill in the final details. Some of them looked thoughtful as the plan unfolded, but the mention of forty squadrons of air cover put everybody in high good humour. Such an umbrella had not been possible prior to this raid.

There were so many Canadian troops embarking at Newhaven on August the 18th that No. 3 Commando had to queue outside the docks in the street for half an hour. The people emptied their houses and, sensing the importance of the occasion, watched us in dead silence from the kerbside. I heard only one remark spoken. A woman looked at Charlie Head.

"*There's* a tall one!" she said.

Charlie later told me that, as a result of this remark, he spent the whole of the raid crouching down, self-consciously sure that his excessive height would make him a choice target.

We boarded our landing craft and prepared for sea. I was travelling in the steam gunboat with my headquarters. She was fast, but most vulnerable, laced with steam tubes which could be punctured by bullets or shell fragments. Owing to their air reconnaissance the Germans knew that something was imminent, and this made it essential for us to leave after dark. We had just time to hit our beaches before first light.

The steam gunboat set out at ten knots with the twenty small landing craft following behind, like ducklings after a mother duck. An hour later breakdowns began among the landing craft. By two in the morning, three craft had fallen out with engine trouble. The Guernsey lesson was repeating itself.

I had just awakened from a nap and was standing on deck, having left all my equipment below. I strolled toward the bridge. Of a sudden, star shells burst over our heads. The ship's Captain said:

"My God! Now look out!"

The shells made day out of night. I could see all our landing craft on our tail and, about half a mile away, five ships which announced their identity almost at once by pouring on us a stream of forty-millimetre and small arms fire. A destroyer had been detailed to escort us but, for the first and last time in my wartime experience, failed in her duty. She had found travelling with us at a slow ten knots too dull, and had dashed off friskily into the night. Now, when she was desperately needed, she was nowhere in reach. The German ships were forming an escort for a small convoy which was proceeding on a normal run from Boulogne down the Channel, and our meeting with them was a pure coincidence. Roger Keyes, who still kept in close touch with our affairs, told me afterwards that our radar had picked up the Germans as they left Boulogne, but there was a breakdown in communications and the warning of their presence never reached us.

The German ships teamed together most efficiently. They chose the gunboat as their principal initial target. She made a gallant effort to return the fire but, within seconds, all her armament was knocked out. I was busily engaged in ducking and weaving to avoid tracer shells which I could see coming straight for me. It is said that you cannot hear the report of the bullet which is going to hit you, but you can definitely see the tracer which is coming straight at your head. I was continually able to evade these tracer shells. I was lucky. Only a few small fragments from the bursting forty millimetre shells hit me. I seemed to be alone on the deck. A naval officer on the bridge saw my plight.

"Come on up here!" he yelled. "The bridge is armoured."

I did not hesitate to accept his kind invitation.

When I reached the bridge I saw that the armour-plating was not preventing considerable carnage. One of the naval officers was quite windy. He kept shouting:

"This is the end! This is the end!"

I was inclined to agree with him. I blew up my Mae West and undid my boots. All around me the bridge was piled up with dead and wounded like a collapsed rugger scrum. There must have been ten casualties there, all hit when looking over the top of the armour-plating.

One officer, whom I knew to be of considerable naval experience, stood with his head and shoulders exposed and directed the ship. Then I saw him fall to the deck.

"I'm hit!" he groaned.

He was bleeding where a shell splinter had penetrated his skull. Brutally, I pushed him upright again. I felt he was our last remaining hope.

Then I noticed that the gunboat was slowing down. By now it was holed like a sieve, particularly in the engine room. Steam hissed like a thousand snakes out of the pipes. I felt helpless, thinking the boat must sink and that there was nothing I could do about it.

The landing craft had scattered in all directions and there was none to be seen. Dawn was breaking but we were beyond sight of land. There was a slight haze on the water and nothing was visible in it. I knew that some of the landing craft had been sunk, perhaps all of them. Then I saw a small boat push through the haze towards us. It was one of the missing landing craft and I could make out Charlie Head and Lofty King standing up and waving towards us. I shouted:

"Come on board, Charlie!"

And he did. We had a consultation and I told Charlie to tend the wounded. In civilian life he had been a veterinary surgeon and he set to work. His first act was to get a large jar of rum from the gunboat's stores, and then the ship's first-aid kit. He did what he could with the many terrible wounds and gave each man a large shot of rum. I helped morale by telling the wounded that Charlie was a doctor. By the time the last man had been attended to they were the happiest bunch of casualties I had ever seen. Leaving all the wounded in the gunboat, which no longer seemed likely to sink, the rest of us piled into the undamaged landing craft and headed for Dieppe. It was now broad daylight. After about an hour we found the main anchorage. I reported to General Roberts in his headquarters ship. I found him in a mood of the deepest depression.

"It isn't going at all well," he told me of the raid. "No. 4 Commando has done their job, but little else has gone according to plan."

There was nothing I could do to help him with the handful of men I had available. I had to hang around for the rest of the day watching the spectacular air battle and feeling useless.

Quite unknown to us, four of the landing craft had shot straight ahead in the early stages of the sea battle. Three of them, under Captain Wills, landed near the eastern gully, and disgorged men on the beach. Captain Wills decided to attack the guns. Corporal Halls took the initiative to charge, and silence, one of the two machine-gun posts on the beach. Others dealt with the second, but before *it* was silenced Lieutenant Loustalot of the U.S. Rangers was killed. He was the first American casualty in land warfare in Europe in World War II.

Heavy machine-gun and mortar fire from other guns situated inland finally pinned down the rest of this group in the gully, just off the beach. Then the Luftwaffe took a hand at dive-bombing them. Fighting went on to the last man while the landing craft made several heroic but fruitless efforts to rescue the wounded. Sergeant Connolly tried to swim out to these

COMMANDO

craft but returned to shore exhausted. Only Lance-Corporal Sinclair managed to reach the landing craft and returned to Britain. The other survivors, all of them wounded, were made prisoner.

At the western gully, Peter Young arrived with the one remaining landing craft and but twenty men. Officers with him were Captain John Selwyn and Lieutenant Buck Ruxton, the originator of the scheme to blow up the German Embassy in Dublin.

"We landed very quietly," Peter told me later. "We arranged with Lieutenant Buckee, who commanded the craft, to wait for us if possible, but told him if he came under heavy fire from the cliffs he was to go off and we would make for Dieppe."

Young and his men found the gully choked with wire. They climbed up the cliffs around it. This took forty-five minutes. During this time the battery started to fire on the main anchorage. Young's party made their way cautiously through the village. They learned that the battery was of four guns and was manned by about two hundred men. Young made two of his men cut the telephone wires connecting the village to Dieppe. Most of the village inhabitants waved to the Britons, then hastily shut their doors as if they expected bullets soon to fly. Three men ran by hauling a woman in a handcart.

"What's the matter?" one of Young's men asked in French.

"She's been hit by a bomb," one of the Frenchmen replied.

They came abreast of a church and just then a German light machine gun opened fire on them. Lieutenant Ruxton, standing his ground, returned fire with his tommy gun. He was joined by Captain Selwyn and others, and the party pushed on into the churchyard. The German machine gun was no longer able to sight on them and ceased fire. Young now reformed his party behind the church. He decided to put their Bren gun and a couple of snipers into the tower and hold the area, but when they searched for a way up the belfry none could be found. Young was desperately eager to engage the battery and keep it out of the main Dieppe battle. He tried to approach it through orchards at the north-west end of the village, thus outflanking any posts guarding the rear approach to the battery. In the orchard he and his men came under rifle fire. They managed to creep up to within two hundred yards of the battery's guns.

At this range they opened fire on the battery. The German's now turned one of their big guns on Young's party and began firing it at a slow rate. Fortunately, the gun could not depress far enough and the shells whistled over the heads of the Commando troops and burst about a mile away. Small arms fire was buzzing angrily in both directions.

For the next three hours our party continued to harass the battery. They were so successful, changing their positions from time to time and beating off all opposition, that the guns never fired again at the anchorage. Finally, the time came to re-embark and the party made their way back down the gully with rifle and machine-gun fire following after them. Lieutenant Buckee was there to receive them.

When they arrived back in Britain, Young and Buckee received immediate awards of the D.S.O. John Selwyn and Buck Ruxton were awarded M.C.s. Further, I was glad to learn from Cross's troop commander that he had honoured his promise to me by standing fully exposed throughout the battle, pouring magazine after magazine of Bren-gun fire into attacking E-boats from his landing craft. All this made me feel better in spite of my own bad luck in being kept out of the thick of things.

On returning to Seaford late at night we started the task of checking up on the casualties. A very efficient search had been made by the Royal Navy and rather more men had been picked up than I thought possible. One tragic feature of the operation was the death of a fine young officer called Peter Kenward. He joined us on the 17th August, embarked with us on the evening of the 18th, and was killed in his landing craft at 4 a.m. on the morning of the 19th.

In the landing craft commanded by Sergeant Clive Collins the naval crew were all killed or severely wounded. Clive managed after some time to get the engines working and, finding himself alone with a crew of dead and wounded men, set a course for England. The compass in the landing craft had been shot out of action, but Clive used his army prismatic compass and fetched up at Newhaven at ten o'clock at night, a considerable feat of navigation. He continued to serve with the unit right to the end of the war, being commissioned in the field while we were in North Africa.

Captain Joe Smale was in charge of a landing craft which sank, and all the men took to the sea. A few more were picked up but there was no sign of Joe. I wrote to his mother a few days later telling her that I must regretfully presume that he had been drowned. Mrs. Smale wrote back a most cheerful letter saying that Joe was a very strong swimmer and that she was quite sure he would turn up. Two months later I heard from a prisoner-of-war camp that Joe had swum seven miles to the beach with the help of his Mae West, and had landed near Dieppe at four o'clock.

After Dieppe fell in 1944 I spent many hours walking round and looking at the position from the German side. Without a doubt our No. 3 Commando landing could have fully succeeded if a proper number of men had been safely delivered on the beaches. On the central sector I do not think the Canadians had any chance at all. They were a fine division but were not at that time battle-trained. They were called on to make a frontal attack against very skilfully sited concrete defences, and the attack was not preceded by any proper bombing or barrage.

I also made careful investigations into the security question, both from the local inhabitants and from some Germans who had been in Dieppe in 1942. The Germans told me that, whereas their reconnaissance aircraft had, of course, continually reported a concentration of shipping at Newhaven, there had been no indication at all of the date or destination of the raid.

Chapter VIII

WEYMOUTH AND GIBRALTAR

OUR LOSSES at Dieppe had been very heavy, amounting to nearly a third of the unit. Morale was quite unaffected and I did not receive any requests from officers or men to leave us. We set to work at once to rebuild the Commando.

By this time the Commando Depot at Achnacarry, Scotland, was a very live place under the direction of Colonel Charles Vaughan, a tough guardsman. Charles at once set about the task of providing the necessary officers and men to bring us up to strength. He was in a particularly good position to do this, as he had just finished training a batch of six hundred volunteers from the police.

This intake of police was perfect Commando material. The men were big, strong and intelligent and had all their police discipline and training behind them. They were real volunteers, keen for the contest. I had 120 of them posted to No. 3 Commando. This was the best single intake we ever received, and every man was a potential leader; many of course were later commissioned and others exerted a fine influence as senior N.C.O.s. We also received excellent officers. Roy Westley was one of these, of medium height, dark and active. Another was Michael Woydevodsky. Michael had a few Russian characteristics and an occasional blue mood, but was a first-class fighting officer and a fine athlete.

We remained at Seaford for the time being. Miss Birley's dance took place and was a great success. I remember at the end of the dance our very quiet Administrative Officer, Captain Martin, usually a man of few words, arguing with Charlie Head, who was trying to fix transport home for everybody.

"I don't want to go home," Martin was saying.

Bill Lloyd was sitting in a nearby truck when a charming girl jumped in and sat on his knee. They all liked Bill.

The man who had vanished with the cash was brought up for trial by court martial. This court martial took place upstairs in the room next to my office, so I could hear what was going on. Colonel Lord Sysonby, commanding No. 12 Commando, was presiding. Roger Wakefield from our Brigade Headquarters was prosecuting; he was a peacetime barrister. The case went on rather a long time and Lord Sysonby was looking forward to a luncheon which I had promised him. Roger Wakefield slipped back into his peacetime mode of speech and kept saying to Lord Sysonby, "My lord, my lord." Lord Sysonby finally became exasperated, and, before adjourning the court for luncheon banged the table and said to the court:

"I know I'm a bloody lord, but for heaven's sake cut that stuff out."

In Combined Operations Headquarters a new plan was evolved to operate on the Cherbourg peninsula. The object was designed to bring on another air battle as this phase of the Dieppe operation had been highly successful. I went to London to study the project and was not impressed. I really thought this would be the end. We had moved to Weymouth so as to embark at Portland for this new raid. When I got back to Weymouth with plans for the operation, Charlie Head met me at the station in his usual good form. I said to him:

"Have you made your will? If not, you had better see a solicitor tomorrow morning."

We started rehearsing and went hard at work to make the best of what I considered a bad job. By the end of October, No. 3 Commando was again as good as ever and possibly a little better. Fortunately, the Cherbourg peninsula project was abandoned.

I knew that a good many of our officers were due for promotion and in spite of the casualties had not always the necessary vacancies. I used to urge them to take promotion to other units, but they were all reluctant to leave No. 3 Commando. One officer had been senior troop commander for a long time, and in the end accepted a posting as second-in-command of No. 6 Commando, who were then under orders to operate in the North Africa landings. He was killed on the first day of the Algiers landing, leading a point-blank attack on harbour installations in Algiers. After this I never urged officers to take any appointments, leaving them to make their own choice.

Weymouth was a good station, with excellent training areas. We worked hard by day and played hard in the evenings. My constant urging of all my officers and men to make No. 3 Commando the greatest unit of all time, sometimes caused this to become a kind of catch-phrase. One night Charlie Head and I went to a dance with the Royal Tank Corps at Lulworth, nearby. The conversation had previously switched from the theme of the greatest unit of all time to that of the greatest girl of all time. While I was dancing with a girl, who perhaps did not quite merit this epithet, Charlie Head, never loath to pull my leg, came up to me and said:

"What's this? The greatest girl of all time, I suppose."

To this I was able to reply with some truth: "No, but she's the greatest dancer."

One of Charlie's virtues as Adjutant was that he was always able to pull my leg and criticise me in private with great good humour, while maintaining a rigid attitude of high discipline when anyone else was about.

Sam Corry, our Medical Officer, had been killed at Dieppe and a young fellow called Ned Moore joined us to take Sam's place. Sam was a very hard man to follow and at first we were not quite sure about Ned. On one of the rehearsals for the Cherbourg peninsula project I fell over a hedge in the dark, finishing up unconscious on a tarmac road many feet below, cutting myself and injuring my jaw severely. I had to go back to Weymouth and at the end of the exercise sent for Ned to come and see me. He fixed me up efficiently but when I complained of a twitching in my jaw he said this was not due to my accident but late hours and a rackety life. I was not feeling at all well and this put me in a bad temper so I sent for Charlie Head and told him I thought he had better get a new Medical Officer. Charlie, with his usual judgment of character, talked me out of this and Ned remained with our organisation to the end, winning two M.C.s. I may say that he was entirely wrong in his diagnosis as I was invariably in bed by ten o'clock and was leading a quiet life at that time.

The local military authorities at Weymouth were none too sure about us but were a great deal better than those at Plymouth. We co-operated with them freely and tried out all their defences at Portland. Naval co-operation, as always, was first-class and we continually did landings on nearby beaches.

About this time I saw in the local newspaper that Superintendent Nat Thorpe of the C.I.D. had arrived to investigate the Piddletrenthide murder. Piddletrenthide is a small village just outside Weymouth. I got in touch with the local police and left a message asking that Nat should look in and see me. We wanted to thank him for catching the man who had taken our cash. He arrived at the flat which Charlie Head and I were sharing, in very good form at about 8 p.m. the same night. We took him out to a place of entertainment and as we came up to the bar I saw Nat giving the barman a very hard look. Shortly afterwards Nat slipped out to telephone, and it transpired that the barman was a well-known confidence man. Nat told us to keep clear of this place; I never heard what happened to the barman.

In November, 1942, while No. 3 Commando was stationed at Weymouth, their traditional rivals, No. 4 Commando, were stationed nearby at Winchester. Lord Lovat was then commanding No. 4 Commando and we arranged a series of sporting events between the units, these being boxing, football and cross-country running. Charlie Head and I thought we had everything in the bag, except football. At this game we had no chance at all as Lord Lovat's team was really good. I told Charlie to arrange something and left it at that.

We had signallers with radio sets at all the events, and other men wrote up progress reports on blackboards. In this way the spectators at each event could tell what was going on elsewhere. I started with the cross-country running, and after seeing that our team was well on the way to winning, moved on to the rugger; this was also going well, and with some apprehension I went over to the football match. As I might have expected, No. 4 Commando were leading by three goals to nothing at half-time. To my great surprise, however, No. 3 Commando made a recovery in the second half and drew level with their opponents. With five minutes of the game to go, the score was three all. By this time I had completely lost my voice through shouting, and in the last few seconds our outside left nodded one in to make it a four-three win for No. 3 Commando.

It was not until several days later that Charlie Head confessed to me that he had sent a false football team to meet No. 4 Commando on their arrival at Weymouth, and to invite them to have a beer or two if they so wished. They took advantage of the offer. Our real team were strictly confined to barracks and had been briefed by Charlie "to win, or else."

The return event took place at Winchester a fortnight later. No. 4 Commando won the football by ten goals to nothing.

Just before Christmas, 1942, we had one of our rare occurrences of serious crime in the unit. The culprit was a pretty hard case who might have been an exception to prove the rule that a criminal is no good in war. Of course I knew nothing of his record; had I done so he would never have got within a mile of No. 3 Commando. Charlie Head unearthed the details of this man's villainies and he was duly charged, brought in front of me, and remanded for court martial, his offence being too serious for me to deal with. He was lodged in the guard room at Portland, then, as now, considered to be a pretty difficult place from which to escape.

On the 22nd December we sent the whole unit on leave but, as life in Weymouth was good, Charlie and I decided to stop in the town.

We were enjoying ourselves on Christmas Eve when, at about eight o'clock a message came that our culprit had made good his escape from Portland. We had no soldiers of our own to help us as they had all gone on leave, but Charlie at once got in touch with the police and with the army authorities at Weymouth. The Colonel and Adjutant of No. 3 Commando spent the rest of their Christmas Eve peering into trains, looking into cafés and generally trying to prevent our man escaping from the district. Finally, at about midnight, the man was picked up on the narrowest piece of Portland peninsula, which has been fatal to so many escaping criminals over the years. The difficulty of the Portland escape is that a man must get through this narrow neck, which is of course well patrolled on occasions when it is known that a prisoner is at large.

We were getting a little restless and were anxious to operate again. It seemed that the home front was played out, as all the planners were scared by the casualties at Dieppe. Obviously, the Mediterranean was the place for us, and I kept pressing Bob Laycock, our Brigade Commander, to send us out there. In mid-January, 1943, Bob told me that we should be leaving the following month for Gibraltar and then the Middle East.

As a final token of respect for the people of Weymouth, we decided to give them an outstanding church parade. It was, when it took place, the smartest, most impressive church parade I have ever attended. Our 120 police added to the picture of military precision by their size and bearing. There was one small hitch. Charlie Head had arranged for the service to take place in the main church. I had never been there. When the parade was quarter of a mile under way I suddenly realised I didn't know where we were going. I made an urgent signal for Charlie to come up beside me.

"Where's the church?" I asked in a whisper.

He looked at me in surprise.

"*I* don't know: I thought you did."

I was very nearly in a panic. There I was, leading five hundred men on a special parade with half the population of the town watching, and I didn't have the faintest idea where to lead them. Luck came to my rescue. Just as I was most worried, we rounded a corner and a large church loomed in front of us. The door was open, the approaches were lined with people who seemed to be waiting for someone to enter. I took a chance and led my five hundred men through the portal. I was right. I doubt if I have ever felt so relieved.

After some leave, the time came for us to go to Glasgow for embarkation. My rule on such occasions was that the men could have a good night out, if they wished it, on the eve of their departure, but any signs of celebration on the actual day of leaving was strictly forbidden and was punished by returning the offender to his unit. We liked our departure to be in keeping with the high reputation of No. 3 Commando. On this occasion, return to unit would have meant a further sojourn in England, and the morale of No. 3 Commando was such that this sentence was dreaded more than ever before. When we arrived at Weymouth station, one man was found drunk and was marched up in front of me on the platform in proper orderly-room style to receive the sentence of return to unit. The R.S.M. ordered the right turn; Charlie Head stepped forward and whipped off the man's green beret, and he was marched out of the station. This was our usual custom; once a man was returned to unit he was no longer entitled to wear the green beret.

At Glasgow we embarked in the transport ship *Letitia*.

Before leaving the Clyde we had lifeboat drill. The Chief Officer addressed our troops, saying that the lifeboats would be for the use of the ship's company, as they were difficult to handle, and that in the event of the ship being torpedoed our men would be better off on Carley floats, which were cork rafts. Our men scarcely appreciated this kind thought as they had been handling boats for two and a half years and were experts at it. However, we had to accept the ruling. The submarine menace was in full swing, as some of us knew only too well from experiences in the Atlantic. Charlie Head and I selected a Carley float and hid in it a bottle of whisky, which we had brought from Weymouth for this purpose. The bottle was retrieved and consumed on arrival in Oran.

We made a wide sweep out into the Atlantic, and for the first three days it was very rough. Many of the men were seasick and the troop decks were not very inviting. On the first day out I went down there with Charlie Head. After looking round for a minute or two, Charlie seized a broom and bucket and went to work. Within a couple of minutes he had all of us, including the sick men and his Commanding Officer, doing the same thing. It was a fine demonstration in the art of leadership. We held a boxing tournament on board and found a new heavyweight, Corporal Dennis, from the police intake. He was a little bit slow on his feet but when he did connect his opponents fell on their faces and were out for a long time.

The ship went straight through the Straits of Gibraltar to Oran, as most of the units aboard were destined for North Africa. A signal arrived ordering myself and Charlie Head to go by air to Gibraltar and we left at once, leaving Peter Young to bring the rest of the unit. Ronnie Tod was in Gibraltar with No. 9 Commando, which we were due to relieve. Charlie and I had an uproarious evening with Ronnie, at the end of which he handed us a very cleverly written letter, giving us the low-down on all the leading personalities in Gibraltar. During our stay on the Rock, Charlie and I added to this from time to time. Our remarks were more than frank. When the time came for us to leave, Charlie left the list with a reliable messenger, to be handed over to Jack Churchill commanding No. 2 Commando, which was due to relieve us. By some mischance, how-ever, Jack lost this list, which came into the hands of the man whom Ronnie Tod, myself and Charlie Head had most freely criticised.

Our role in Gibraltar was to launch seaborne raids on various installations in Spain, should Hitler decide to occupy that country. I at once started looking over the admirable plans which Ronnie Tod had made for these projects. All would have been comfortably accomplished, the main problem being to leave and return to the fortress of Gibraltar under fire from the guns on the mainland.

No. 3 Commando arrived a couple of days later. Everybody on the Rock was pleased to see us, and they were rather astonished to see the turn-out and saluting of our men, as turn-out discipline in general had become a little lax among the garrison on the Rock, many of whom had been shut up there for two years. Everywhere No. 3 Commando went I insisted absolutely on the greatest possible cleanliness and attention to detail, both in battles and in the peaceful periods between. A clean and tidy soldier feels better and works better. In the severest battles our men always shaved and washed if a drop of water was available. A wash and shave had nearly as great a stimulating effect as a good meal.

We started at once to train for the projects planned for us. The situation was curious as Germans on the mainland of Spain were watching everything that took place. I used to retaliate by taking leave to Spain on frequent occasions and having a close look at the places we might need to attack. Also I took a good many trips in aeroplanes, flying along the three-mile limit, briefing our officers. As I was briefing Peter Young one day in a Hudson we had borrowed for the afternoon, he asked to fly once more past the place he was planning to attack. As we went by for the second time he tapped me on the shoulder and said:

"That's enough. . . . 's a piece of cake."

Bill Chitty had been captured at Dieppe and Lofty King was in charge of our police. He didn't have much work to do as there was very little misbehaviour. We had to send one man to the detention barracks for fourteen days, but Lofty told me later that this man on his first Sunday of freedom had gone back to have tea with the warders, so we decided that the atmosphere of the detention barracks was too friendly and did not trouble them any more.

Sometimes the expeditions to Spain got a little uproarious as the sherry was cheap and the food good, so the parties tended to develop. One Sunday Charlie Head and I came back to the border with very dry mouths. There were, as usual, beautiful oranges on sale at nominal prices. We quickly bought a few of these and although we were in one of the Governor's cars, neither of us could resist the temptation to start in on the oranges. We drove back to the Loretto Convent where we were billeted and a few minutes later the telephone rang and an A.D.C. from Government House told Charlie that a disgraceful thing had been seen, namely two of our officers sitting in the back of the Governor's car sucking oranges. Charlie was fully able to cope with this. He asked the A.D.C. to come and see him at once and then gave this young man a most severe lecture, saying that a ridiculous mistake had been made, that the officers in question were the Commanding Officer and Adjutant, and furthermore that the Commanding Officer was a friend of the Governor and would undoubtedly secure the A.D.C.'s dismissal if this allegation was not withdrawn. A speedy withdrawal and apology from the A.D.C. followed. As a matter of fact I did know the Governor, General Mason MacFarlane, and spent many delightful evenings with him, enjoying his wonderful Spanish food and wine and talking about the Fortress and the old days in India, where he and I had served in the same stations.

Just beyond the Loretto Convent there was a steep cliff rising about 300 feet, and I used to take my daily exercise by climbing it. Until this time I had never been frightened of heights. One evening, however, I had climbed half-way up and suddenly felt sared stiff. I managed to complete the climb, which was not a difficult one, and for the good of my morale had to do it a few more times, but since then I have never been any good at heights. Jock Allen, a large and amiable Scottish sergeant, was constantly climbing about the rock face with Bill Lloyd and our other climbing experts. On one occasion a young and inexperienced officer slipped and fell while several hundred feet up on the north face of the rock. Jock Allen calmly lassoed him and dragged him to safety: for this he received the George Medal.

Our boxing team cleaned up the Gibraltar championships. There were 20,000 men on the Rock and we had five champions; in several cases the finals were between two men from No. 3 Commando. Corporal Dennis, our heavyweight, landed a colossal knock-out on one of our new officers, who came to after more than two minutes and tried to continue the contest. Johnny Dowling had put on a bit of weight with the good Gibraltar food and had to work off about ten lbs. before his fights. Normally he enjoyed his boxing so much that he went the full three rounds, never attempting a knock-out. This time he was not feeling so good after his weight reduction and landed a knock-out in the first round; until this time we had all thought of him as a boxer only.

In mid-April the time came to move on to North Africa. As usual the orders for the move came at short notice and we had to put in a hard day's work getting everything ready. Our padre, by my orders, always attended our morning parade, and although he attended that morning he did not hear of our move, as nothing was said on parade owing to security regulations. We sailed at midnight that night minus the padre, who had contrived to spend the whole day in a small place like Gibraltar without getting to know that his unit was moving.

CHAPTER IX

L'AFRIQUE DU NORD

WE SAILED from Gibraltar to Oran in the fast ship *Princess Emma*, which had been our sister ship on the Lofoten expedition. At Oran we trans-shipped into a large landing craft and sailed for Algiers. Everywhere we saw pre-war French tourist posters advertising the charms of "L'Afrique du Nord." This sounds much more attractive than "North Africa," but on the whole we did not find the country romantic.

After the atmosphere of Gibraltar the arrival at Algiers was an unpleasant shock. There was nobody to meet us and certainly nobody to help us. After prolonged investigation I found that we were destined for a camp about ten miles west of the town at Fort de L'eau.

We went to Allied Force Headquarters in Algiers. This was the worst and most depressing headquarters in my experience. I had to deal with a senior staff officer who was a classic example of the pompous, obstructionist type often met with in the early stages of the war. One day he asked me to luncheon. I arrived punctually at his headquarters, which was shared by the British and the Americans. I was told to wait. Much later he came downstairs.

"Oh, Slater," he said, "our luncheon is off. I'm having mine with General ———."

A group of American officers overheard this remark. They kindly offered to take me to luncheon with them, at the same time making it clear that they deplored the bad manners and ill-breeding of their English colleague.

"They aren't all so bad," I felt impelled to say.

"We know that," my host grinned.

With Peter Young, I went to General Eisenhower's planning H.Q. in a village schoolhouse three miles south of Algiers. Colonel Anthony Head had just come from London to help the planners and we were shown into his office by a young officer who must have thought we had already been briefed about the plan to invade Sicily. Head was delayed about half an hour. The plan for Sicily was laid out invitingly on his desk and I took the opportunity of looking it over. I was shocked by it.

"This is one of the worst plans I have ever seen," I said to Peter.

It called for innumerable small, dispersed landings all around the south and east coasts from Palermo to Catania. I saw by the intelligence summary that there were two first-class German divisions with armour attached and a very large number of Italian troops on the island. My impression was that the Germans had arranged for their forces to be very mobile, so that they could meet attacks where they came. I was sure our plan of dispersed attacks would fail.

Naturally, when Colonel Head arrived, I failed to mention that I had been studying the highly secret plans on his desk.

"The role of No. 3 Commando," Head told me, "would probably be to go in and capture one of the batteries covering the beaches."

This information enabled us to start training on the proper lines. I am sure that if I had been able to discuss the plan with Head he would have agreed wholeheartedly with my criticisms. Later I heard that he had made constant efforts to bring sense to the rather curious planning team then assembled at Algiers.

I went once more to Allied Force Headquarters to try and get some transport and make some general administrative arrangements. The same staff officer I had met before greeted my arrival with:

"I can do very little for you. I can't find you any transport. I can't tell you when you are going to operate; you will just have to wait around in the transit camp."

After this I swore I would never go to Headquarters again. General Eisenhower had not had time to check on his subordinates. Never before or since have I ever struck anything so bad. I told Charlie Head he would have to do the work with Headquarters. Charlie was much more successful. He got an introduction to a very senior officer and said to him:

"No. 3 Commando are engaged on a top-secret project. Only Eisenhower and my Colonel know the full details. I know you won't ask me to talk about the operation, but we must have some transport."

Immediately a flow of brand-new transport began, and in a couple of days I had to tell Charlie to stop it as we had more than enough for our needs.

We managed to keep the depressing atmosphere from affecting the unit. Peter Young organised a three-day training scheme in the Atlas Mountains, and we got our boxing team going. A local training unit thought they were good at boxing, but were speedily disillusioned. Johnny Dowling won his fight easily and Corporal Dennis applied his usual knock-out. An American heavy-weight in Algiers was challenging all comers to a fight for five hundred pounds. I told Charlie Head to raise the money in the Commando and to back Dennis to beat him. We put Dennis into strict training.

The food in our camp was adequate but dull, and I was always anxious that our soldiers should do as well as possible. I got to know that excellent Algerian wine was obtainable in a country district, and sent our Signals Officer off to buy a large quantity. I gave him a truck and told him not to stop until he had gone forty miles, and then to buy sufficient wine for our 500 officers and men. He came back in the evening with a huge barrel containing 500 litres, or 1,000 pints, of good red wine, for which he had paid £5. Everybody enjoyed their evening meal.

As the negotiations for Dennis's fight with the American reached a climax orders came for No. 3 Commando to move on and join the Eighth Army.

We had an extraordinary journey by rail to Terbessa. The track had been opened up quite recently and the carriages were of very old-fashioned design. No. 6 Commando had been badly shot up from the air while travelling along this track some months previously and their engine driver had stopped the train and run off when the first hostile aircraft appeared. I made sure this would not happen to us. We had two former engine drivers in No. 3 and I put them in the engine to keep the civilian driver company. The sanitary accommodation on the train was of the most primitive nature and I had to forbid my men from using it. Instead, we had to rely on stops. Since the stops came at irregular intervals, the windows had sometimes to be used in emergencies. The trip took four days in all.

The first two days were relatively uneventful. Whenever we stopped, Arabs appeared like magic, offering eggs for bully-beef. While this trade went on, other Arabs sneaked around to the far side of the train in an attempt to steal blankets, rifles or anything else that appealed to them. One of these desert dwellers made the mistake of trying to take Lofty King's rifle while Lofty was looking. Lofty grabbed another rifle, shot the culprit and jumped out to retrieve his own weapon.

On the third night I was awakened from sleep when the train came to an abrupt stop. I sent Charlie Head out to investigate, and in a moment he returned.

"The train has broken in half," he said.

He added that we were in the front half and that the back half was out of sight. Returning to my blanket, I told Charlie to do whatever was necessary to rectify the position.

The next thing I heard was a loud argument between Charlie and the French guard. One of the accomplishments Charlie did not have was a sound knowledge of the French language.

I heard Charlie saying, "Piston? Piston?" believing that he was repeating the words of the guard. Charlie thought that the engine's pistons had failed. Actually, the French guard, who was highly excited, was using a somewhat similar word. What had happened was that the lack of sanitary accommodation had resulted in an unfortunate accident which the guard thought was deliberate. When the train stopped he had run outside to see what had happened to the missing half. His face had been an unintentional target. I had to get out of bed and search for a solution to this small international incident, but the guard refused all further duty. He insisted that the French nation had been slighted. In the circumstances, I don't think I blame him.

While we were stopped the engine was uncoupled and sent

back to find the missing half of the train, which it did. No. 3 Commando was together again.

The next day was, I think, the happiest of my life. An Eighth Army staff officer was at Terbessa station to meet us.

"We are delighted," he said, "to have a Commando with us. We've heard a lot about you."

The contrast with Algiers, where no one had cared, was wonderful. For fourteen years as a regular soldier I had suffered from the atmosphere of pompous staff officers who invariably said "no" and stifled all initiative. There had been the stultifying military obstruction of Plymouth, and most recently of Algiers. From the moment we joined the Eighth Army, everything was delightfully different. We were looked after and administered as if we had operated throughout the desert campaign with them. Nothing was too much trouble. Everybody was courteous, helpful, efficient. The Army took its tone from its Commander, and Monty's influence spread right down to the lorry drivers who would always stop and give you a lift. Anyone who tried to get a lift from a lorry driver in Algiers would be there still.

It was decided that we should move to Alexandria by way of Tripoli. We left at once for the transit camp at Tripoli. On the first night in this camp we had no transport except for a motor cycle. Peter Young was bringing the unit transport from Algiers, and as all the vehicles were new, was taking things easily. After dinner I saw Charlie Head in the mess and said I would drive him into Tripoli on the motor cycle. I have some experience of these vehicles, having taken part in a few pre-war races and competitions. I should not be surprised if I still hold the record from Charing Cross to the Royal Military Academy, Woolwich, which I covered in twelve minutes dead on a Sunbeam motor cycle at 2 a.m. in the autumn of 1927.

We drove into Tripoli at a leisurely pace, sitting very properly upright. In Tripoli we met Major John Hopwood of the Black Watch, an old friend of mine, who was recuperating from a severe wound suffered in the desert campaign. We had a most cheerful evening and then decided to return to camp. On this return journey I demonstrated to Charlie some of the technique of motor-cycle racing. We flew down the road, myself lying flat on the petrol tank and Charlie crouching over me. A lorry appeared, coming in the other direction, and we had to take to the sandy verge of the road. The Colonel and the Adjutant bit the dust in a pretty big way, both shooting over the handlebars. Neither of us was hurt.

After ten days at Tripoli, we left for Alexandria in a rat-infested and highly inefficient transport ship. I have been in many ships and have always been happy in them, but this was the exception. The condition of this ship was alarming. On her next trip she was sunk by a torpedo with considerable loss of life. When I heard this news it did not surprise me at all.

We moved into a camp a few miles from Alexandria and I went with Charlie Head to Cairo to meet General Dempsey for the first time. The General had established a small planning headquarters run by his 13th Corps, which was to launch the initial assault in Sicily. By this time Monty had altered the original Sicily plan so that his attack would be a more concentrated assault on the south-east corner of the island. Dempsey took a good look at me when I entered his office.

"Have you done any of these Commando operations, Slater?" he asked.

"Yes, sir. Guernsey, Norway twice, and Dieppe."

I could see I had still made no impression. I was to learn that Dempsey liked to take his time in judging people.

Dempsey was running the Sicily planning temporarily while Monty finished the North Africa battle. He gave me the specific details of No. 3's job in the assault. We were to be put ashore on the flank before the main landings so that we could soften up beach defences and capture a battery to fire along the landing area. This would give the 5th Division a better chance of getting ashore with the minimum trouble. Our landing was to be made a few miles south of Syracuse, and the battery we were after was three miles inland, in an olive grove behind the village of Cassibile. The beach which the battery covered was of great importance to the 13th Corps, as the brigade to be landed there was to help the Airborne Brigade in the capture of Syracuse, on which the entire army plan depended.

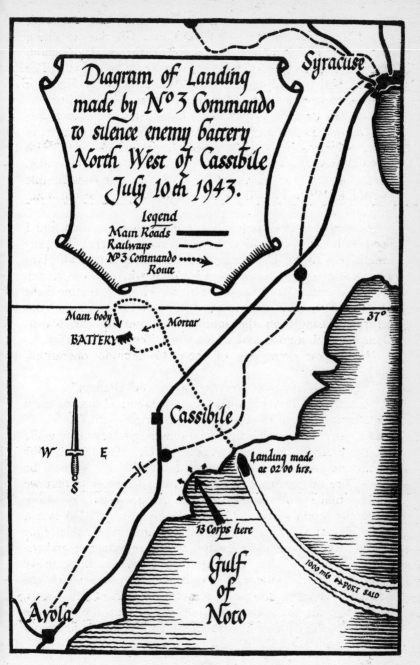

Diagram of Landing made by Nº 3 Commando to silence enemy battery North West of Cassibile July 10th 1943.

Legend
Main Roads
Railways
Nº 3 Commando Route

Syracuse

37°

Main body
BATTERY

Mortar

Cassibile

W   E
S

Landing made at 02.00 hrs.

13 Corps here

1000 mls ➤ PORT SAID

Gulf of Noto

Avola

I decided to lead the attack on the battery myself with half the Commando, leaving Peter Young and the remaining three troops to deal with the pillboxes and beach defences. General Dempsey told me to study the plan carefully and to tell him how long it would take us to do our jobs. No. 3 Commando, in addition to their operations, had carried out so many arduous training schemes that we knew exactly the capabilities of our officers and men. We had experimented against all sorts of fixed defences at Plymouth, Weymouth and on the Clyde, and so knew to a minute how long it would take us to do our work. After studying the plan with great care I told General Dempsey that we could put the battery out of action in ninety minutes from the time we touched the beach, and that Peter Young would deal with the pillboxes in forty-five minutes.

"Right," the General said, "carry out your final training and I'll come and see you in a week's time."

There were a good many administrative arrangements to be made in Cairo. We found that other headquarter establishments there were by no means up to the Eighth Army standard. Even at this stage of the war no work was done from 2 till 5 p.m. At 5 p.m. a leisurely start was made, and at six o'clock Egyptian butlers started circulating with trays of whisky and soda. Nobody put away any of the secret papers while these men were serving the drinks, and we were worried about security.

I decided to move No. 3 Commando to Suez as the vessels which were to take us to Sicily were lying in Suez Bay and we wished to start training with their landing craft. The Railway Transport Officer at Alexandria, who arranged our move, was typical of the worst of his type. A mistake had been made in the signal sent to him from Cairo, giving our numbers as 250 instead of 450. I noticed that this signal was sent off at about 8.0 p.m., when the whisky was probably doing its work. The R.T.O. would not believe that we were really 450 strong and provided us with a diminutive train which he refused to enlarge. As we expected to travel through in a day we all got aboard. The trouble was that we had a great many heavy stores and after we had loaded about half of these I noticed that the springs of the baggage van were sagging very badly. Railway officials all over the world invariably spot this and we were desperately anxious not to have a hold up. I put the matter to Charlie Head who solved the problem immediately by erecting tea buffets opposite each spring, and these buffets continued to supply tea until the very last moment. When the vans were fully loaded, instead of being U-shaped the springs were completely reversed. Three times on the way to Suez the train ran over, and killed, Egyptians—otherwise the trip was uneventful.

At Suez we built a dummy battery at exactly the right distance from the sea and reproduced as many of the features of Sicily as we could. We held twelve full-scale rehearsals, trying out every single detail. Each man knew the number of paces from the beach to the forming-up place, the compass bearing for each leg of the advance, and every detail of the plan. General Dempsey expected our best, and he was going to get it. After he had come to see us in training, I knew I had him on my side. He saw my attack on the battery fully rehearsed, and then saw Peter Young demonstrating his technique on the pillboxes.

"I shan't have to worry much about you," he said. Monty came to see us too, and appeared just as satisfied with our work. I was very proud of the unit. It made you feel good to have fellows like Monty and Dempsey pleased to have you with them. No. 3 Commando was the first Commando to operate for Monty, so we were particularly anxious to do well.

Conditions in our camp were bad and the number of flies was unbelievable, in spite of desperate efforts to keep everything clean. We had been warned against raids into the camp by Arabs in search of arms, and I was determined that they should get none of ours. On about the only night that we did not rehearse, I fell into a very deep sleep and suddenly woke up, shouting to Charlie Head, who shared my tent:

"Go on, Charlie, the Arabs are here." Charlie leapt up with his pistol in his hand, circled the camp, and, seeing no one, went back to report to me and found me once more in the deepest slumber. My vivid dream is still quite clear in my mind.

As Derby Day approached Charlesworth, my batman, asked my permission to make a book. I gave permission with the usual proviso that the book should be absolutely straight and that starting prices should be laid. Unfortunately for Charlesworth, the Egyptian paper gave "Straight Deal," which won at 100-6. There are no laying-off facilities in the Suez desert, and Charlesworth was left with a liability of £160. He came to consult me and told me that his total assets were £85. I acted as a one-man Tattersall Committee and ordered him to settle for half, so that all winners received half of the money to which they were entitled. Everybody was satisfied and Charlesworth took his beating very well.

Major Walter Skrine, a most efficient staff officer from Combined Operations, asked if he could join us and I was delighted to have him. One day he and I went to Cairo to get some official documents and have another look at the air photographs. I gave Walter the papers to look after and we left for Suez. It was a very hot evening and we stopped for a drink at a roadhouse half way between Cairo and Suez. We continued our journey, and, being tired, I went to bed soon after we got back. First thing in the morning I sent for Walter and asked him for the papers, which he produced, but found that one document was missing. Fortunately this did not concern anything very vital, though it had been marked "Top Secret." A couple of hours later a security man arrived at our camp producing the missing document, which Walter had dropped outside the roadhouse. A court martial became inevitable, the only question being whether Walter or I should figure. We made a careful, factual report of the whole matter and Walter was selected as the victim. We motored up to Cairo together, Walter to be court martialled, and myself to give evidence: I was not exactly happy. The verdict was guilty and a severe reprimand. Never for one second did this affect our friendship, which lasts on the same level to this day.

A couple of days later, in early July, 1943, we embarked. My party was in the *Prince Albert*, a tip-top ship which had taken No. 4 Commando on their successful Dieppe venture. Peter Young had the rest of the unit in the *Dunera*, a large transport ship. He was to do his separate landing and to join us at Cassibile after completing his work. The *Prince Albert* soon sailed for Port Said. We were ready to sail for Sicily.

At Port Said a signal arrived from General Dempsey:

"I have already told you how delighted I am to have No. 3 Commando in the Corps, and of the confidence I have in them. I congratulate all ranks on the magnificent state of the unit."

We felt very proud to have established ourselves in the Eighth Army and were determined to prove our operational value.

As an appendix to this chapter, here are my notes on my C.O.'s Conference which was held on the 15th June, 1943:

Place: Orderly Room. All Officers, less sick.

Rehearsal Stage.

1. All men to know scheme and be tested.
2. Loads to be tested.
3. Sick. No border-line cases will go on the job.
4. Examine loads. (It is no good saying it will be all right on the day.)
5. Get rid of idlers and grousers. One went yesterday.
6. Admin. Canvas buckets, for letting down on toggle ropes into wells.
7. Speed. . . .
8. Reloading mags. Practice required.

Briefing Stage.

1. Men half-briefed already. Brief from models in small groups. Be fully briefed yourself first. Time with models usually limited. Check bearings, paces, etc. for yourself. Two short periods with models better than one long one.

Operational Stage.

1. This is where the officers earn their pay. Algy Forrester's performance at Vaagso, by going like hell down the main street, really won that battle. You can't just say, "Nip along there. I'll be along in a minute."
2. Boat discipline. You are in charge in all respects.
3. Be ready to bump into an enemy at sea; we could have done a hell of a lot more firing on the last show. (Dieppe.)
4. Never be satisfied until mags are refilled. (4 Troop.)

L'AFRIQUE DU NORD

5. All officers must think at least two stages up in rank. (At Vaagso, Sgt. White, D.C.M., from corporal became Troop Commander.)

6. The morale side is directly concerned with the officer's side. None of "The men are too tired to do any more"; it usually means "The officer is too tired."

7. Fullest detailing of posts, pickets and guards. No. 1 Troop's demonstration.

8. Keep getting information back.

9. Every officer is to be able to speak on wireless. Budd to have a set near mess.

10. Right or wrong. One real chance—take it in both hands. One moment is the right one. When in doubt go in.

11. Discipline. Take every opportunity to wash, etc.

12. If there are bars in the ship this is no time for boozing. Plenty of sleep is what's needed. Have what's going if it's there. Have two or three drinks. No parties.

13. Be correct to civilians and P/Ws. Proper requisitions for horse and cart, etc. If he's a farmer he's probably a decent chap and he can get it back later.

Chapter X

SICILY

IT WAS good to get under way, heading back into Europe. The *Prince Albert* was another cross-channel steamer fitted with eight landing craft; in the bows of each landing craft we had mounted a Vickers K machine gun. The purpose of these guns was to engage the beach defences. They were light weapons with a great fire power, and each magazine carried 100 rounds. We carried out our final briefing with the help of a model which the R.A.F. in Cairo had made up for us from their photographs. Everyone was happy and confident.

George Herbert and Clive Collins had been commissioned while we were in North Africa and rejoined us from the O.C.T.U. just before we left. They settled in well as officers.

I had one rather dubious officer who had been posted to me by a very high authority in London. I never liked this fellow, and half-way to Sicily he came to me and said:

"I'm sorry, Colonel, it's no good, I'm windy."

I said: "You ought to have thought of that before, you'll land with us and like it. I shall be watching you personally."

As we approached Sicily, in the late afternoon, we could see the top of Mount Etna. The sea had become very rough, and it seemed impossible to achieve a surprise attack, but the troops were singing and laughing as if this were just another exercise run-in. Ten miles out we transferred to small landing craft. There was a good deal of confusion and ships were going in all directions. The *Sobieski*, a large transport, appeared on our port beam, going very fast and heading straight for us. A large ship appearing out of the dark like this is most alarming, but she just missed us. Darkness had now come to cover us.

After a while I was not sure that we were heading in the right direction. A canoe marker boat, launched from a submarine to aid navigation, was flashing its pre-arranged signal, but I could see the dark zig-zag of mountains against the skyline and recognised their outline from the careful study I had given to maps and photographs. With these landmarks I could see the canoe had drifted with the strong wind and tide.

"I think that boat's in the wrong place," I said to Lieutenant Holt, the Flotilla Commander.

He agreed and went on steering strictly to the compass. When we came to a destroyer, he hailed her:

"Can you give us a course to the Scoglio?" The Scoglio was a prominent rocky feature near our landing place.

"Bearing 268 degrees," was the answer.

Very soon we saw the big, rocky feature, standing almost perpendicular from the surrounding country, two hundred feet high and fifty yards in diameter, a natural pillar of rock. When we were a couple of hundred yards from the beach, a stream of machine-gun fire came at us from a pillbox. We replied with the Vickers K guns mounted in the bows of each landing craft. Very soon the fire from the pillbox stopped. It was manned by Italians who, at this stage of the war, seemed easily demoralised.

I had briefed Lieutenant Holt to put me on the beach first, but at the last moment I saw a boat coming in with a late spurt on the outside. It was Charlie Head who wanted to beat me for the honour of being first man into Sicily. He didn't quite make it.

The other boats landed their men. We were faced by masses of wire and many pillboxes, all useless unless manned by determined troops. We were soon through.

We formed up a hundred yards inland, exactly as we had practised. I crouched down to tell my batman, Charlesworth, something, and our faces were inches apart when a tracer bullet flashed between our noses. We both reared up like startled horses. Neither of us spoke.

Then the firing stopped. The country was flat and open with a high stone wall dividing the fields every few hundred yards. We started our advance, preceded by two scouts fifty yards ahead of us. It was a bright moonlight night and now everything was still. We were the only ones ashore.

"Get those scouts moving a bit faster," I said impatiently to John Pooley.

This was no reflection on the courage of the scouts; after a landing in a strange country, they were apt to go a bit slow. Soon, still not content with our speed, I went to Pooley again:

"Look John: let's get out in front together. Unless we're quick that battery'll be firing on the main landing."

I was uneasy. I had promised General Dempsey to do the job in ninety minutes.

We went ahead, and I flashed a shaded torch continually back into the advancing column. The object was to show everybody the direction of our advance. It saved time as all they had to do was to keep moving in the direction of the flashes from the torch. We were moving in double file at a good speed. I could hear the occasional dislodgement of a stone or the shuffle of feet, that was all. My men were heavily laden, each of them carrying a ten-pound mortar bomb in addition to his other equipment. We had no transport, and this was the only method of getting a good supply of mortar bombs forward. There was little talk; just necessary orders, and few of them were needed. The stone walls were four to five feet high. At times the mortar men with their especially heavy loads were hard put to keep up with the column.

"This is nice and quiet," I whispered to Pooley. "We might be on a training scheme."

We came to a farmhouse. After I passed it, the farmer rushed out with a shotgun and fired at one of my men. Later, Curly Gimbert remarked:

"Sorry we had to shoot that farmer. He was a good chap. He had the right spirit."

Just after this I heard the battery firing. This made me doubly anxious to get to work. We reached a dry river bed which ran in front of the battery and I detached a party of ten men to crawl up it and harrass the battery from the front with a two-inch mortar and rifle fire. Meanwhile, the three-inch mortar was sited exactly along the line of guns, four hundred yards from them. Each man dropped his mortar bomb as he passed the spot. Four Bren guns were also placed here. In a few minutes we had the battery under devastating fire, both from the front and the left flank. Lieutenant Roy Westley commanded the flank party.

All this time the rest of our party was forming up in the rear of the battery, two troops up and one centrally in reserve.

"The assault is going ahead in five minutes time," I said over the wireless to Westley, and to Sergeant Fraser who was in charge of the party in the river bed.

From time to time Fraser's men shot parachute flares over the battery. Our assaulting troops then poured in heavy additional fire. When the flares died down we resumed our advance. Charlesworth sounded the Advance on his bugle, and we went in for the final assault. We came to barbed wire and blasted paths through it with bangalore torpedoes, long metal tubes filled with explosive. We dashed through the gaps firing from the hip. I was using my Gerand. I was fond of that weapon. Finally we used the bayonet. The Italians stuck it fairly well until near the end, replying to our fire with automatic weapons. When we had cleaned them up, we proceeded to blow up the guns. Some enthusiast, just in the spirit of clean fun, also decided to blow up the ammunition supply of the battery, about one thousand shells. It was a very loud bang. There was plenty of stuff flying and it was a very foolish action, but no one was hurt. The battery was blown up eighty-five minutes after landing, redeeming my word to General Dempsey with five minutes to spare. Of all the operations in which I took part, I enjoyed this the most. It was carried to a successful conclusion without a casualty.

I decided that everybody had better have something to eat and told Charlie Head to post sentries and to give the Commando an hour to get a meal inside them. I found that Charlesworth had already got his spirit stove into action, and having obtained some eggs from a nearby farm, he soon had a first-class breakfast ready for me. Everybody else also did themselves well. As we were finishing this breakfast we heard another Italian battery firing from a position two miles away. I said to Charlie, "Come on, we'll go and deal with that one, too." As we moved off we heard the beginning of a tremendous bombardment of this battery by the ships of the fleet, so decided to leave well alone.

We then moved to Cassibile as arranged. While we were waiting there, Charlesworth and Lofty King, both ex-bandsmen, dug up some musical instruments, a trumpet and a bass drum, and began to entertain us. A Scottish regiment entered the town from the beach with the piper playing. The Jocks thought they were first into the village. It must have come as a shock to them to hear "The Same To You" from the trumpet and the drum.

Peter Young arrived with his party from the beaches. He was in a bad mood, as his landing craft had been indifferently handled and had put him ashore late and in the wrong place. There were some Italians holding out in a fort nearby and I gave him permission to capture this place. He came back in the evening much more cheerful.

On the evening of the 11th July we moved into the hills on the left, to act as flankguard for the army. It was quiet up there and we had a good rest. Next day we re-embarked in the *Prince Albert* so as to be ready for further seaborne operations. The ship's company of the *Prince Albert* assembled on deck and gave us three cheers as we approached. Praise from the Royal Navy was always very welcome.

On the 13th July I received a signal to go at once to Syracuse to meet Monty, General Dempsey, and Admiral McGrigor, to plan another operation. I had barely time to warn my men that they would be operating that night when I was whisked away in a fast motor launch for the meeting. As we left, a Messerschmitt dive-bombed a tanker a few hundred yards away. The tanker went up with a terrific roar, flames reaching several hundred feet in the air.

The meeting took place on the quay at Syracuse. It was very hot, and most of the buildings had been bombed. The battle was going favourably and the three senior officers were in high spirits. Dempsey, who did most of the talking, began:

"We've got a new operation for you tonight. It's an ambitious one, but I think you'll like it."

Then he unfolded the details of the job. Monty aimed to push right on to Catania in one bound. Only one road ran from Syracuse to Catania and he wanted to cut this at two points so as to disorganise the one and only main line of

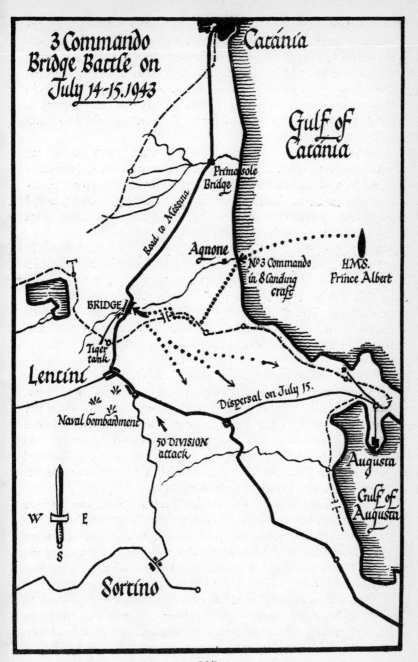

3 Commando
Bridge Battle on
July 14-15.1943

Catánia

Gulf of
Catánia

Primasole
Bridge

Road to Messina

Agnone

No 3 Commando
in 8 landing
craft

H.M.S.
Prince Albert

BRIDGE

Tiger
tank

Lentini

Naval bombardment

50 DIVISION
attack

Dispersal on July 15.

Augusta

Gulf of
Augusta

W   E

S

Sortino

communication of the Germans and Italians with their bases. There was to be an airborne drop to seize and hold the Primasole Bridge, a few miles from Catania. No. 3 Commando was to land ten miles behind the lines and advance seven miles inland to seize the Punta Dei Melati, a bridge over the Leonardo River, two miles north of Lentini. Monty's intelligence men, usually unerringly exact, said that only Italian opposition was likely to be met on the beaches. They knew of no German troops in the vicinity. I have an instinct for danger and was not so sure. That bridge was on the only road linking the German and Italian armies with their bases in the Messina area. It seemed likely to me that Jerry would want to make sure it was well guarded.

Before I left, Monty had a last word:

"Everybody's on the move, now," he said, full of energy. "The enemy is nicely on the move. We want to keep him that way. You can help us do it. Good luck, Slater."

I felt that it was a bold gamble which would probably come off. I didn't mind taking gambles for Monty and Dempsey. We should be out on our own with no one to help us, and it was up to us to look after ourselves. Just before leaving, General Dempsey said to me:

"If, by any chance, 50 Division, who will be our leading troops, don't get through to you by first light tomorrow morning, clear off and hide up for the day."

The landing was to take place at ten o'clock that night at Agnone, a small village seven miles due east of our bridge. I hurried back to the *Prince Albert* and we sailed at once. This left us only a couple of hours for issuing orders and briefing the men on this highly complex operation. No air photographs were available and we wouldn't have had time to examine them if they had been. We had to organise our landing in two flights, as the landing craft available could only take half the Commando at one time. Everybody took the briefing well, and even the officer who had been windy on the way to Sicily, seemed to be in better spirits. I told him to come with me in my landing craft and to bring a bangalore torpedo so as to make the first gap in the wire. Half way to the place where the landing craft were to be lowered, a German E-boat appeared and fired two torpedoes at us. The Captain went full ahead and the torpedoes passed close under our stern.

Again our transfer to Lieutenant Holt's flotilla of landing craft was carried out smoothly. Before we hit the beach a concentrated crossfire was opened on us from several pillboxes. We returned the fire heavily, but, surprisingly, the enemy continued his machine-gun attack, unlike the wilting fire during the earlier landing. The whole place was lit up with tracer bullets which passed angrily in the air from both directions. A sailor was shooting from just behind me so that the muzzle of his weapon was only a few inches from my head. Holt shouted:

"Don't shoot the Colonel's bloody head off!"

I found it all most exhilarating. There was a bright moon and we could see men running about on the beach. Johnny Dowling was standing beside me firing magazine after magazine from the Vickers K gun. Streams of tracer were flying in all directions. The noise was too great for me to make myself heard, so I was slapping Johnny's face to indicate to him which way to switch his fire. We continued in good formation and hit the beach.

This time, however, Holt overdid my instructions to beach my boat first. He put me on shore at least two lengths clear of all the others. The officer carrying the bangalore torpedo was keen to redeem himself and tried to follow me out of the craft, but in his anxiety he got the bangalore jammed across a three-foot ramp leading from the boat, and the press of men behind him caused a serious hold-up. I was left nakedly alone on the beach for what seemed a very long time. The sand boiled up around me as the bullets struck. Somebody also started throwing grenades down the cliff at me. I thought the bullets were enough without these extras.

At last the other boats were beached. With a cheer the men went to work on the wire. Holt's flotilla returned to the ship for the rest of our troops. I did not see the second flight land, but I heard later that it was just as noisy a party as ours had been. As Lieutenant Holt's craft pulled away the second time, almost beyond range of shore, he was hit in the neck and killed.

Very soon after we passed through the wire, some men from No. 3 Troop brought me back a prisoner to view.

"Lieutenant Herbert has sent back this prisoner for you, sir," a lance-corporal told me, very correctly.

I looked at the prisoner. He was in German uniform. This was George's effective way of telling me that there were Germans about. It also explained why the opposition on landing had been so stiff.

I caught up with Peter Young, who was firing a Bren gun against a German machine-gun position. Walter Skrine was spotting the effect of his fire. The German machine gun fired back, and Walter received a long burst through his left leg. He asked me for morphia and I called up Ned Moore, the doctor. I told Ned to fix him up and to attend to the other wounded on the beach.

Over the next mile, through the village of Agnone, we had a series of violent little battles. We had to advance continually against machine-gun posts. In one foray, George Herbert was knocked unconscious by an exploding grenade. He was bleeding from one ear. He seemed to recover consciousness.

"How are you, George?" I asked anxiously.

He groaned. "Getting weaker," he said.

George thought he was done for, but fortunately he had just had a temporary concussion. In ten minutes he was on his feet and leading the advance in his usual fighting, forceful style. Peter Young, Charlie Head, and Lofty King were also operating in magnificently aggressive form. We passed Agnone station, and just as we did, Captain Tim Leese, the Commander of No. 1 Troop, was shot through the eye. Then, suddenly it seemed, we ran out of all the trouble.

It was then, in the freshly quiet night, that I heard the drone of many aircraft. Very soon they were overhead and down through the night bloomed at least a dozen parachutes. This small party of men, British parachutists who had been dropped by mistake on their way to attack the Primasole Bridge, fell amongst us. Many others flew on to be dropped later according to plan. A corporal from the bunch which had been dropped early was brought to me.

"This Primasole Bridge is a hell of a long way away," I pointed out to him. "You'd better come along with us."

"Sorry, sir," he said, shaking his head, "I've got my orders."

And he set off with his men for their objective, many miles distant.

I was now leading the way along a railway line. It was easier going here. We walked in double line, one file on each side of the tracks. It was absolutely quiet now, and there was little cover for an enemy ambush. I felt reasonably secure, for I imagined that the enemy had his troops on the roads. I called a short halt for a troop commanders' meeting, and to check up on casualties. We had left thirty men behind on the beach, giving us a strength of 160 officers and men. John Pooley was in the second flight an hour and a half behind.

I said: "We'll continue the advance with No. 4 Troop leading, then No. 3, then No. 1, with Headquarters in front with No. 4. For God's sake don't straggle: we're going to cover about three miles of rough country before we strike the bridge. We must push on fast to get to it before the enemy's main retreat."

We struck across country, leaving the railway line behind. We found ourselves in rocky, low hills and forced our way through bramble thickets and over stone walls. Then we came to the Leonardo, about a mile below the bridge.

"It looks shallow to me," Bill Lloyd said. "I'll try it for depth." He jumped in, and disappeared under water. He scrambled out again.

We tried several other places and at last found a ford, waist deep. I thought it important to cross the river first and come in on the defendants of the bridge from the unexpected north. Now we passed through olive groves, moving quietly and easily. Then, 250 yards ahead, I saw the bridge, white in the moonlight. I could make out four pillboxes at our end of the bridge but there was no enemy soldier in sight. A lorry crossed, its lights dim, its driver confident that there were still ten miles between him and the nearest Allied troops.

We paused there for five minutes so that the unit could form up. It was nearly midnight.

"All right," I said, "No. 4 Troop go ahead."

It was up to Bill Lloyd and his men to clear the pillboxes. I went with him. We walked along the road together. The night was as still as it would have been in the heart of Cornwall. Then Lieutenant Brian Butler, commanding the leading section, rushed each pillbox with his men, throwing grenades which split the silence with their reports.

There were shouts and loud groans. I turned to Lloyd.

"Well, they're Ities anyhow, that's a good thing."

The pillboxes at our end of the bridge were all cleared in ten minutes. The position was quickly consolidated and we made our dispositions for the events to come.

The ground was like concrete. Despite our efforts it was not possible in the time available to dig proper defensive positions. The best we could do was to make use of the cover of the concrete works constructed by the Italians, mostly pillboxes.

We settled in, and I thought we had done well to get there. We were out on our own, ten miles ahead of the Eighth Army, right across the enemy's only line of communication.

I was anticipating a record bag of prisoners, and told Charlie Head to find a suitable place to put them in. After a short time he came back and took me to a nearby hut. I am afraid I spoke to him sharply:

"We're going to have hundreds of prisoners, not dozens, Charlie. Pull yourself together and find a proper place."

Very soon the first Italian prisoners came in. One of them was shouting and screaming, giving our position away.

"Knock him out," I said to Charlie.

Charlie couldn't do this in cold blood, but Lofty King came up and soon silenced the Italian with a terrific uppercut.

I was feeling tired after our long march. All was still again. I told No. 3 Troop to occupy the far side of the bridge. Then, with my haversack as a pillow, I had a little snooze. I woke up very shortly to a loud explosion very close.

"What's that?" I asked Charlie.

He said calmly: "A mortar bomb."

"Don't be silly," I said, "we haven't brought a mortar."

"No, but they have," Charlie replied.

They had, indeed. For the next few hours they literally showered us with mortar bombs, inflicting many casualties. By the time John Pooley arrived with the second flight, the casualties were mounting, and we had about fifteen killed and wounded. The trouble was that we didn't have enough cover. The pillboxes could take only about a dozen and now our strength was 350 officers and men.

There was a clump of evergreen trees beyond the far end of the bridge. Out of it, unexpectedly, a Tiger tank appeared. It started shooting at us with its eighty-eight and its machine gun. I knew then that we were facing Germans as well as Ities. Later I learned that a parachute company had been quartered in the wood the day before. As I was conferring with Charlie Head in an adjacent olive grove, a branch, sliced clean off by an eighty-eight shell, fell on top of me. A minute later I felt the wind of another shell parting my hair (I had some in those days).

All this time there had been a flow of German traffic, southbound from Messina. As the lorries came we shot them up. I had stationed a troop a hundred yards up the road to deal with such matters, and now the noise was heightened by the bursting ammunition in these burning lorries.

I was upset at the extent of our casualties and decided to take revenge by joining in the game of despatching a few of the Herrenvolk travelling in the lorries. I went towards one which had just been set alight by our gunfire and a huge German came out, roaring with righteous indignation. He caught me off balance. Fortunately George Herbert was at hand and disposed of him with a single shot from the hip.

"You get out of here, Colonel," George said crossly. "There's plenty for you to do running the unit."

At that point another German ammunition lorry arrived. Lieutenant Cave, a young officer who had recently joined us, bravely but unwisely fired his Piat into it at pointblank range. An enormous explosion followed, with Cave in it. He died shortly afterwards.

A mortar bomb which burst at his feet, badly wounded Bill Lloyd just after this, fracturing both his ankles so that the bones of one protruded from the flesh. Lofty King found a bicycle and propped Bill up on it.

"If you've never seen a man ride a bike with two broken legs," Bill said bravely, "look at me."

He rode off, assisted by two men, to continue in the battle. Some time later still on the bike and still helped by the two soldiers, he led an attack on a German machine-gun post and was killed. This was my most serious personal loss of the war. Bill died fighting mad. He was a quiet man normally; courageous but unspectacular. He died in a spectacular way.

Sergeant Hopkins, a regular soldier and a King's shot had two fingers shot off his right hand at about the time Bill was first wounded. He walked back to Lofty King, waving his hand, which was streaming with blood.

"That's the lot, Lofty," he said. "I'm finished with shooting now."

He didn't realise that he had received two severe chest wounds. He died of them later that night.

I decided that we had got to do something about the tank and sent for John Pooley. I pointed out a house which was a little in front of our position.

"John," I said, "get your Troop into that house and see if you can shoot up the tank. You may be able to reach it with your Piat mortar."

As I was talking to him, mortar bombs were falling around us and John kept diving to the ground. He said afterwards that he thought I was very brave, standing up and not diving every time the mortar bombs burst. I had done plenty of diving earlier on, but had got tired of it and had decided that there was just as good a chance standing up.

John Pooley went off with his Troop in extended line and we gave him covering fire. The tank opened up with its machine gun. I was horrified to see the entire line fall together, then breathed again when they picked themselves up. They had merely fallen over a trip wire which, fortunately, had not been mined. A moment later they were in the house and, using it for cover, fired heavily on the tank with their Brens and a Piat. Unfortunately, the Piat, which could have knocked the tank out, was just beyond its effective range.

The bridge was about 120 yards long. Eventually No. 3 Troop, moving under it, were half way to the other side. Then the German paratroops lining the far bank began to shoot down on them. Taking whatever cover the bridge could give them, they held out for about an hour on the other side of the river. Then I ordered them to withdraw. Of sixty men, eight were casualties. While they were under the bridge they managed to remove demolition charges which the Germans had laid. By this action they saved the bridge from being blown up.

The plan was that the 50th Division was to fight their way to relieve us by first light, about 4.30 a.m., but they did not arrive, and it was not until later that I learned they had been held up in a major battle near Lentini. By now, too, another battle was under way six miles to our north at the Primasole Bridge, between our airborne forces and the Germans. From time to time the fleet took a hand, bombarding Lentini. It was a noisy morning. At first light I saw there was little hope of holding on. I decided to move to hilly country to our west from which I hoped still to dominate the bridge, at least for a while.

We started to move, troop by troop. Now our training and discipline proved their values. One section climbed the first hill in extended order, accurately pursued by airbursts from the tank's eighty-eight. A shell burst over the middle of the section and a man dropped, but the rest were unhurt. This revealed that our dispersed formations, on which we had insisted during training, actually did minimise casualties. Another shell-burst, directly behind him, seriously wounded Charlie Head. When he fell, Lofty King picked him up and started to carry him along with the rest of us.

"Drop me and go on," Charlie said to him. "I wouldn't do this for you."

Lofty stopped dead in his tracks.

"No," he muttered, "I don't believe you would," and continued to carry him.

They were two big men; they made quite a lump together.

We reached the railway line again. The fragments from the airburst shells made nasty sounds, ricocheting from the lines and metalling. Shortly we were established, however, in a good position on the hill. The tank had crossed the bridge after us and got busy sweeping the hill with its machine gun. I called for another troop commanders' meeting.

"It's obvious," I said, "that 50 Division can't reach us. There's nothing more for us here: we must get back. Our only chance is to split into small parties. Lie up where you can during the day and make your way back to our lines tonight."

Then I walked over to talk to Charlie Head. He and my batman, Charlesworth, were too badly wounded to move off with us. We hid them carefully in a house.

"Best of luck, Charlie," I said, hating like hell to leave him, "50 Division is sure to be here this afternoon."

Charlesworth was not hit quite so badly as Charlie, although neither could walk. I told him to look after Head.

Charlie grinned.

"We'll be all right," he assured me.

He looked very ill just the same.

I moved off with my party, which included George Herbert, Brian Butler and Peter Young. Peter and a few others soon left us as the party was too big for concealment. We had not gone far when we saw a good place to hide in during the day. It was in some thick olive groves. To reach the groves we had to cross a large field of ploughed land. Before getting to the field we came to a small tomato garden. They were the best tomatoes I have ever eaten. We moved on, and as we stepped into the field George Herbert spotted some men beyond the far edge. He peered at them through his glasses.

"They're Germans," he said.

I looked at them through my own glasses.

"They're not," I said. "They're some of our own men."

We continued on our way. When we were in the middle of the field, with no cover, the men opened a heavy and uncomfortably accurate fire on us.

"You're right, George," I yelled, and started running.

The ground was dry and every bullet kicked up a little cloud of dust, but we kept going and finally got out of the field and behind the crest of a small hill. Just then we saw more men ahead of us.

George said: "Now we *have* had it. Don't be a bloody fool any more, John. Let's pack in."

But this time I was right. They turned out to be John Pooley and a party from his troop. We all got into a very deep ditch and lay down, except for George, who moved around cautioning the men against smoking or talking. We resigned ourselves to wait until dark.

I lay on my back at the bottom of the ditch, envying the Spitfire pilots returning from their missions. We had no quick

COMMANDO

way of getting back. I thought the old game was getting very rough, and wondered how the rest of the unit was getting on. I also thought that it was not such fun being hunted, and that if I ever got out of this alive I would not go hunting or shooting again. Brigadier Charles Haydon, in our early days, had often told us that commanding officers must have long periods of quiet thought and contemplation, and I had a splendid chance on this day to carry out his instructions.

From time to time, parties of enemy soldiers came our way. They didn't, however, look in the ditch. Had they done so, they would have had a very warm reception. The day passed quickly and, when night fell, we left the ditch to continue our ten-mile march to safety. The first two miles, through olive groves, were the most tiring: we were bent double all the way as the branches were thick and low. When we came to the Agnone-Lentini road, we were challenged by an enemy post just as John Pooley dashed across the road.

"Give us some covering fire!" I yelled to John.

It was another bright moonlit night, and I saw him throw his last grenade with great accuracy to the door of the post. It failed to explode. We ran across the road in groups of two or three. Each time there was a brief burst of enemy fire. Again we were lucky and none of us was hit. The rest of the way was plain walking, but plenty of it. Finally we reached an Eighth Army anti-aircraft position. The last thing I remember before falling asleep was George Herbert draping a borrowed great-coat over me.

After a few hours sleep we started the task of collecting No. 3 Commando together again. Small parties were scattered over the countryside, having undergone similar experiences to our own. Charlie Head and Charlesworth were first captured by the Germans and were then overrun again by our own troops. We sent them off to hospital in Tripoli. Walter Skrine was also captured, but was obviously too ill to be moved; the Germans treated him well and we got him to hospital the next day. He had a year in hospital and then started riding horses again, having been a well-known amateur rider before the war. All the operations he had undergone made one leg shorter than the other; he found that this upset his balance while riding and so had his good leg shortened to match the bad one. In 1947 he rode his horse "Martin M." in the Grand National.

Losses had been severe and a good many men had been taken prisoner. Most of these returned to us in various ways. Peter Long, small, dark and taciturn, broke out of his camp in the middle of Germany and got back to England by way of the Pyrenees and Gibraltar. Roy Westley, Michael Woyedvodsky and Charlie Buswell, broke out of their train as it was crossing the Brenner Pass, and walked back six hundred miles to meet us as we came up the coast of Italy. There were many similar escapes. All those who had been prisoner spoke in very high terms of our opponents, the 4th German Parachute Brigade. They were well-fed and well-treated, and said that the training and discipline of the Germans was very similar to our own. In the evening I saw General Dempsey.

"I'm sorry we didn't manage to hold on until 50 Division caught up," I apologised. He smiled.

"You had no chance of doing that. You did a great job. There's no doubt it relieved the weight of the attack on us enormously, you cutting the lines of enemy communications for so long."

The operation was well recognised in the matter of awards. Peter Young got a Bar to his Military Cross, Charlie Head, John Pooley and Ned Moore got Military Crosses, and Lofty King, Johnny Dowling, Sergeant Taylor and Corporal Spears were awarded Military Medals. I got a Bar to my D.S.O.

A little later, after Catania had fallen, Monty called me round to his Headquarters.

"Slater," he said, "that was a classic operation, classic. I want you to get the best stonemason in the town. I want you to have him engrave 'No. 3 Commando Bridge' on a good piece of stone. Have this stone built into the masonry of the bridge."

I was delighted to obey Monty's order; and doubly delighted to hear that Charlie Head and Charlesworth had arrived safely in a British Army hospital in Tripoli.

Brigadier Bob Laycock arrived on the scene with Nos. 40 and 41 Royal Marine Commandos, with whom he had been operating on the south coast of Sicily. No. 2 Commando also arrived from Gibraltar. We were all put under Bob Laycock's command. On his way up Bob had called in to see Monty and had presented him with a green beret which Monty at once put on. Monty and General Dempsey had spoken to him very nicely about No. 3 Commando. Bob said to me:

"I've got an operation coming off in Italy and I'm going to take Nos. 2 and 41 Commandos. I want you to take over Nos. 3 and 40 Commandos and the Special Raiding Squadron, and to operate them as a brigade."

I moved into Bob's Headquarters and handed over No. 3 Commando to Peter Young. Randolph Churchill was running Bob's Headquarters and we lived in great comfort, as Randolph took on a chef from the principal hotel in Syracuse which had been bombed. Randolph was very good company and was a fine soldier in the battle.

Peter Young quickly reorganised No. 3 Commando, but owing to casualties was only able to form three troops. We gave everybody a chance of returning to ordinary duty as we thought some of them might have had enough; only three men decided to go. Everybody knew that the gamble which Monty had taken had been justifiable and they were prepared for plenty more. We were able to do a little recruiting from nearby. No. 13 Corps produced a new Intelligence Officer for me called Allan Peile. He looked very young and innocent, but knew most of the answers. General Dempsey, at this stage, asked me to become a member of his personal mess, which meant that I could go there to dinner whenever I wanted a happy evening. We seldom talked of the war at these dinners.

On the day Messina fell, Peter Young sent Cross and Farringdon, two of our more enterprising soldiers, into the town on a foraging expedition. Farringdon was a keen painter and decided he was more interested in drawing Etna and the beautiful surrounding countryside, and as Cross had meanwhile discovered a fire engine in the town, the two of them motored to the upper slopes of Etna, unwittingly passing through the German lines as they did so. They were caught in direct fire from the German lines, losing both the fire engine and Farringdon's paintings, and were forced into hiding. Eventually they were taken prisoner but escaped and returned to us within a fortnight, when they were greeted by the 13th

Corps Intelligence Officers as escaped heroes. An order was given that they were to appear before General Dempsey to relate their story. I had to do some quick thinking to prevent this, as I knew that the General would very quickly find out the truth. Cross could never keep out of trouble.

Peter Young started a series of reconnaissance landings on the toe of Italy. Three times he went and returned with prisoners and information. On the fourth trip his landing craft was hit by a shell and sank. Peter and his party from No. 3 Commando got ashore, and had to hide up and wait until the main invasion of Italy.

As we approached Messina, Monty decided to launch another operation to trap the Germans remaining in Sicily. The 4th Armoured Brigade was to carry out the operation and I decided to use No. 2 Commando to operate with them. I went as second-in-command of the 4th Armoured Brigade. The landing was to be made about ten miles in advance of the Eighth Army and was directed by General Oliver Leese, commanding 30 Corps. The General's Chief of Staff carried out the final briefing, and as he was starting Monty arrived and said that he would like to listen in. Monty said nothing until the question of air cover came up, when the Chief of Staff said this cover would consist of four squadrons of fighters. Monty immediately jumped up.

"Not enough," he said, "send the whole Desert Air Force." And the whole Desert Air Force it was.

I went back to see No. 2 Commando, who were up to full strength and were longing to operate. Jack Churchill, previously my second-in-command in No. 3 Commando, was their C.O. General Oliver Leese was about to arrive to address the troops, but Jack was nowhere to be found. I had a frantic search made for him and finally found him in a cave carefully packing up his bows and arrows. Jack frequently took these instruments with him on operations, but had decided that this time he would use more orthodox weapons. He was not in the least put out when I told him that the General was already five minutes overdue. He calmly completed the packing and then walked over with me to the assembled troops. General Oliver Leese arrived and gave them a simple and effective briefing.

Captain Faulkner briefed the landing craft crews, and I was very pleased to hear him tell them to drive the craft hard up on the beach. Naval officers, by nature, do not like beaching their boats hard and are apt to lie off a few yards, dropping the soldiers in the water.

We sailed from Catania in tank landing craft. Jack Churchill and No. 2 Commando soon cleaned up the opposition at Santa Theresa where the landing took place. We were about eight miles south of Catania. I landed with Brigadier Curry, commanding the 4th Armoured Brigade. We quickly came under heavy shell fire and it was certain that the Germans had an observer hidden near us. Every move was followed by shells, even though we were well-concealed from the German positions in Sicily and on the Italian mainland opposite. I spent an hour lying under a tank with Brigadier Curry. Shells were falling all around us.

"This is no good," said Brigadier Curry, "let's move to the railway station."

One of our batteries was in action in the railway yard. The observer at once followed us up and got a direct hit on one of the guns, killing all but one of the men serving it. This man ran round screaming at the top of his voice, and I shouted at him to shut up as hysteria is not good for morale. As I finished shouting he dropped dead at my feet. I felt deeply ashamed of myself. We were about to move forward so Brigadier Curry told me to arrange for the burial of the dead men. As no padre was available I had to conduct the service. I was made unhappier by the fact that I was not carrying a prayer book and had to do it from memory.

This was the only occasion throughout the war on which I controlled a shoot by a section of artillery. I found the section in action near Santa Theresa and directed a shoot on to the mainland of Italy. These were the first shells the Royal Regiment fired into Italy, but by no means the last.

Chapter XI

ITALY

BRIGADIER LAYCOCK had told me that after the initial landings in Italy, I should be recalled to England with No. 3 Commando to take part in the D-Day landings. It had always been my ambition that No. 3 Commando and I should have a part in this final combined operation.

One day, just before we crossed into Italy, General Dempsey called me in.

"John," he said, "if I could fix it for you to be stepped up to Brigadier, would you like to remain out here in Italy with the 13th Corps?"

"Thank you very much, sir," I replied, "but I'd rather take my chances in the Second Front when it comes off."

Nevertheless, although I was to remain a Lieutenant-Colonel, the General confirmed my appointment to command a brigade. This consisted of No. 3 Commando, No. 40 Royal Marine Commando, and the Special Raiding Squadron. No. 40 Commando was the original Royal Marine Commando, an entirely volunteer unit, and at that time under the command of Colonel "Pops" Manners. The Special Raiding Squadron, formed from veterans of the desert war, was commanded by an enormous Irishman, Colonel Paddy Mayne. He was an Irish rugger international and had been with the Commandos in the early days. I felt I had a really strong force.

I organised a small but efficient headquarters. Bob Laycock had left me his Brigade Major, Brian Franks, and Basil Bennet joined as Camp Commandant.

Paper work was nil; Brian used to pull a few bits of paper out of his pocket occasionally and write something down. This was our filing system. When Basil was asked to hand over the mess accounts to his successor, he startled this rather solemn young man by telling him that there were none.

We lived very well indeed and every now and then Basil

asked us for a small contribution of lire. These two men now control the destinies of the Hyde Park Hotel and the same atmosphere of efficiency is to be felt there. Alas, the paper work in the hotel is now no longer confined to Brian's pocket, and Basil's minions seem to want quite a lot of lire every time I leave the place.

Allan Peile was the Intelligence Officer, and I took from the Special Raiding Squadron a good padre called Ronnie Lunt. I put Ronnie in charge of all the ecclesiastical arrangements within the brigade. He was shrewd and capable, exactly what we wanted as a padre. He was also tactful. Late one night, after we had had a few drinks, I asked him to name a price against my entering heaven. I was expecting at least ten to one. To my great surprise he told me that I was a six to four on shot, as all my sins were of a healthy type.

In Sicily and Italy the rate of advance was always slowed down by the fact that only one coastal road was available. All the Germans had to do was to maintain a few posts along these roads, each post holding out long enough to cause a considerable delay. General Dempsey said to me:

"I'm going to keep landing you and your force a few miles ahead of us, then we shall be able to get on quickly."

He knew that the Germans, hearing that a landing had been made behind their posts, would quickly retire.

The first of these landings was made by the Special Raiding Squadron at Bagnara, situated near the toe of Italy. Bagnara is the town where from time immemorial the story had been told of the ladies concealing poison in their mouths and giving poisonous kisses to invading soldiers. This was duly recorded in the Eighth Army Intelligence Summary and the men were warned against any sort of philandering. Paddy Mayne effected his landing and after a severe battle captured Bagnara on the 5th September, 1943. The German post retired and the Eighth Army was able to move straight into Bagnara and several miles beyond it.

Encouraged by this success, General Dempsey decided to launch a further seaborne attack on Vibo Valentia, some thirty miles further up the west coast. This landing was to be made by 231 Brigade and our Commando Brigade. General Urquart, later of Arnhem fame, commanded the landing. General Dempsey told me not to go on this operation as General Urquart was fully capable of handling matters and the presence of another Brigade Commander would only complicate things.

No. 231 Brigade and the Commando Brigade landed at Vibo Valentia at 3 a.m. on the 9th September and successfully overcame the severe opposition. By midday the town was in our hands. Another twenty miles of valuable territory had been gained.

Admiral McGrigor, now First Sea Lord, commanded the naval force in person. While surveying the scene, he came close to the shore and was wounded by the fragments of a bomb dropped by a Messerschmitt.

We had a few peaceful days waiting to join up with the Salerno battle further up the coast. The Salerno forces solved their own problem without our help, however, so 13 Corps with the Commando Brigade was told to move to the Bari area on the east coast of Italy. The Eighth Army was moving quickly up the east coast but Kesselring's forces were showing signs of making a stand on the River Biferno, which offered a good defensive position. Monty had decided to outflank this position by making a landing with our brigade two miles north of the river at Termoli, a small town with a useful harbour. With Termoli in our hands, the German armies would be forced to withdraw to the north. The Commando Brigade was moved in landing craft round the bottom of Italy.

I told Allan Peile that we would motor to Bari, so that we could get there first and make the plan. The trip across Italy was intriguing as the country had not been properly cleared of the enemy, and there were interesting possibilities round each corner. The country was hilly and attractive. In each village a crowd assembled as we passed through and gave us a cheer. After about fifty miles our driver overturned the jeep; I remember a large container of red wine spilling its contents over everything. Allan Peile, an expert driver, took over this duty and there was no further mishap.

Bari had fallen to the airborne troops just before we arrived. Allan Peile soon got us fixed up in the best hotel, the Albergo Imperiale. We went to the bar where the Spumanti cocktails were very good and reasonably cheap. Needless to say they had rocketed 200% in price by the next day. After having several of these drinks, I was approached by a lady who had seen the title "Commando" on my shoulder. I learnt that she was on a four-hour parole from an Italian concentration camp and she wanted me to get her released permanently. As she looked pleasant and I was in a good mood, I told her I would be up after luncheon to see to the matter. Allan and I had an excellent meal and I then told Allan to attend to the question of organising our headquarters and getting preliminary details of the Termoli operation from General Dempsey. I also told him to get me a jeep ready at 2.45 p.m. and that I would drive myself. He knew better than to enquire into my movements.

When I got to the concentration camp it was still fully operational with armed sentries at the gates. I had not got even a pistol and the effect of the champagne was wearing off, so I did not feel so good. However, I was in good voice, and gained admittance. My lady was waiting for me, but she turned out to be on friendly terms with the Camp Commandant who was not anxious to see the last of her. Also at three o'clock in the concentration camp she did not look quite the same as at one o'clock in the cocktail bar. Furthermore, many of her companions were better looking than she was. I must admit that at the time my thoughts were a little confused, as several sentries, thinking that I was threatening their Commandant, closed in on me in an alarming manner. I arranged for the camp to be closed down and drove the lady, with some of her compatriots, to the town.

When I got back Allan had a good deal of information for me. Termoli had a garrison of about five hundred paratroops from the 4th German Parachute Brigade, our opponents of the Commando Bridge Battle.

"We're going to have a hell of a battle," Allan said.

I agreed, but was confident we could carry out our task. I felt the operation was a gamble but thought it would come off. We expected to be about twenty miles ahead of the Eighth Army when we landed, and we knew that Monty and Dempsey would make a great effort to catch up with us quickly. We got out an operation order which filled only one sheet of paper. I liked to keep such things simple. An ordinary infantry brigade

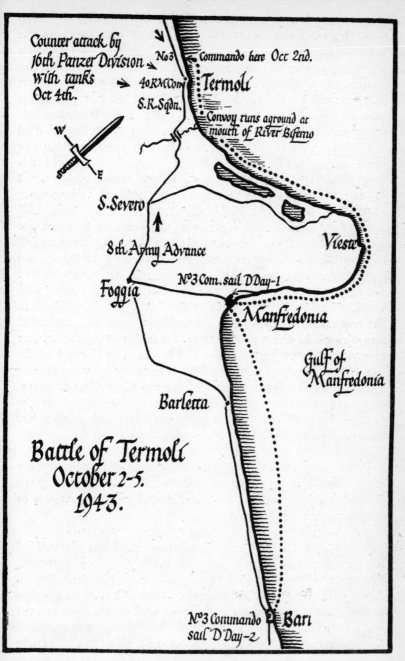

Counter attack by
16th Panzer Division
with tanks
Oct 4th.

No 3   Commando here Oct 2nd.

40 RM Com

Termoli

S.R. Sqdn.

Convoy runs aground at
mouth of River Biferno

W
E

S. Severo

8th Army Advance

Vieste

No 3 Com. sail D Day -1

Foggia

Manfredonia

Gulf of
Manfredonia

Barletta

Battle of Termoli
October 2-5.
1943.

No 3 Commando   Bari
sail D Day -2

would have used at least twenty-five sheets for the same operation. It involved the movement of over a thousand men and
ten landing craft, 120 miles from Bari to Termoli, the capture
of Termoli and the holding of the town until we were relieved.
We had no naval escort, as the navy had not yet caught up
with us. This simplified the naval side of the operation.

We were a well-trained team and I told General Dempsey
that evening that he could rely on us to capture Termoli. I
hoped that the relief would not take too long, as I felt sure there
would be a violent German reaction. Briefly, the plan was for
No. 3 Commando to secure the beach about half-a-mile west
of Termoli. No. 40 Royal Marine Commando was to capture
the town and the cross-roads west of it, and the Special Raiding
Squadron was to pass round the western outskirts of Termoli
and to secure the area south of the town. The Special Raiding
Squadron, like No. 3 Commando, had suffered heavy casualties
and were badly under strength, so I had to ask 40 Commando
to do most of the work. They were a fresh unit, up to full
strength. General Dempsey questioned my decision to use
No. 3 Commando for the initial landing.

"They've had a very severe time," he said. "Hadn't you
better keep them in reserve?"

I wanted to be absolutely sure of the operation, and I knew
that the first landing was not necessarily the most dangerous.
Often it took place before the defences had woken up. Also, it
would be good for my morale to go up to the beach with the
men I knew so well close behind me. I had decided to land
first with our small Brigade Headquarters.

The Brigade arrived at Bari by sea on the scheduled night
of the operation. The men had come in landing craft which
had been inadequately supplied with fresh water. They were
tired and dirty.

"We can't operate tonight," Brian Franks told me. "The
men have had no sleep for four days, and had a very bad
passage. You really must get the thing put off for a day."
He was obviously upset about it.

"I'll get in touch with General Dempsey," I promised.

When I did, the General agreed to postpone it for twenty-
four hours.

Meanwhile, I requested the naval man at Bari for a sailing order, a necessary formality. He was obstructive.

"I'll have nothing to do with this," he said. "I've heard nothing about it and I'll not let you go."

I felt it was not worthwhile arguing the point. Instead, to give us freedom of movement, I decided to establish our own base at Manfredonia, a good port farther up the coast. Brian Franks wrote out the sailing orders to leave Bari and I signed them. We then moved up the coast. This was somewhat irregular, but necessary, since things had moved so fast that we had out-run our naval liaison and I did not wish to become entangled in red tape. Later, after a big explosion at an ammunition dump in Bari, I remarked to General Dempsey that it would have been no great tragedy if the naval man there, who was known to the General, had gone up with the ammunition.

"You mustn't say things like that," he told me. "I don't like that side of your nature."

Manfredonia had not been confirmed as clear of the enemy, so I sent Captain David Barclay, Adjutant of 40 Commando, by road with a party to clear the town and to see that the harbour was ready for us and clear of mines. This was a fairly tall order but he grinned and saluted smartly.

"Everything will be ready for you," he said.

On reaching Manfredonia, David had everything ready for us, and we had a comfortable night in billets. General Dempsey came to see us and we felt rested and ready to operate by the next day which was the 1st October, 1943.

In this out-of-the-way place a large mail arrived, and in my share was a present which has since cost me hundreds of pounds. Back in 1941, Charlie Head and I had entertained a lady and her brother in Scotland, and by some odd chance it was now that I received from her a present of a thousand "Players". Until then I had been a light smoker, and this tendency was encouraged by the awful filth which comprised the cigarette issue to Mediterranean forces at that time. In the stress of the week to come, every one of those "Players" was consumed by myself and my very small staff. From that day I have been a heavy smoker.

Unfortunately, we only had a small-scale Italian chart

for the sea journey. I talked things over with our naval Commander.

"If we're attacked on the way the only thing to do will be to run ashore," I said. He agreed.

Our flotilla slipped anchor at 11.30 a.m. on the 1st October. It was a beautiful day and we sat on deck enjoying the sun and the lovely coastline. Soon after nightfall, however, heavy clouds banked up and it became ominously dark. As we neared the mouth of the Biferno, shallow with silt, but not thus marked on our inadequate chart, the entire flotilla ran softly aground. It was not a comfortable feeling to be aground close to an enemy coast at one in the morning, but the naval crews had us free of mud in half-an-hour.

As we reached our rendezvous, it began to rain. We transferred quietly to the small assault craft, in which Brigade Headquarters and No. 3 Commando were to land. The navy had done a fine job of navigation, and had got us to exactly the right place and at the right time. It was pitch dark, and the rain had stopped. There was a lingering feeling of dampness in the air. The night was dead still. This, the moment before a seaborne attack, with the enemy coastline looming up in the night, was the supreme thrill for me: nothing else could match it.

Our headquarters boat beached first, three quarters of a mile west of Termoli. It was 2 a.m. Brian and I dashed out of the craft. We were followed by four signallers who carried a heavy wireless set on a stretcher. We needed this heavy set, as it had to transmit and receive a distance of at least thirty miles to General Dempsey's headquarters. Another signaller carried carrier pigeons in a basket, just in case the radio didn't work. We climbed the steep sandhills with the four signallers puffing and blowing as they carried the heavy set, slipping now and then and cursing under their breath. Brigade Headquarters was on the move and in action.

Thus far, No. 3 Commando had landed and secured our bridgehead without the knowledge of the enemy. The large landing craft in which 40 Commando and the Special Raiding Squadron were to come ashore had struck on a sandbank which, again, had not been marked on our chart. I turned to a naval lieutenant who had come ashore with us, and pointed out the grounded craft.

"Can you get your small craft going to give them a reasonably dry landing?"

"Yes, Colonel: I'll get cracking."

Soon these troops were passing through us on their way to work, and then the peace became an uproar. Spandaus, Brens, rifles chattered and cracked. Very soon our head-quarters, on a sand dune half a mile from the town, was remote from the shifting battle. There was fighting in the streets now, a lot of shooting, plenty of small stuff sounding crisp and harsh and deadly.

"Let's get on the move," I said to Brian.

In a few minutes we heard an engine making starting noises and, hurrying, found it facing in our direction. Brian and I performed an encircling movement. He jumped into the cab, pistol in hand.

"Hands up!" he said in German to the driver.

The Jerry did as he was requested. His train never did make its scheduled trip northward. The coaches behind the engine were loaded with German troops, fast asleep. We woke them up and made prisoners of them. They took a lot of rousing and could scarcely believe what was happening. They thought they were thirty safe miles behind the front lines.

I had my headquarters set up in the back yard of a house near the station. The radio was just then on the move so we released a couple of pigeons with news of our progress. They merely circled and landed again.

"Those damn Itie birds," said Brian Franks in a tone of complete disgust, "they're no better than their troops!"

There was a certain amount of desultory firing from the Germans in the area of the station now but nothing concerted. No. 40 Commando had cleared up most of the opposition here in the first rush. It was six in the morning. Meanwhile, 40 Commando and the Special Raiding Squadron had moved on. Our opponents were the German parachutists we had encountered before, in the Battle of the Commando Bridge. Some of them seemed eager to fight until they died. I observed one lying in an olive grove partly behind a tree, about eight hundred yards in front of our position. Although obviously wounded—his actions were stiff and unnatural—he continued to fire at us regularly and accurately. We were unable to move anyone forward to take him prisoner. Instead, we returned his fire. He died where he fought, in the olive grove.

During the fighting General Heydrich, the German Parachute Divisional Commander, slipped out of the town on foot. He kindly left his car behind, a 1939 Horsch, long, low, black and very fast. No. 3 Commando found it, cleaned it up, and presented it to me.

It has always struck me as extraordinary how the news of a battle sometimes fails to spread. Throughout the morning, German supply lorries kept coming in from the north. No. 40 Commando ambushed twelve of these at a northern cross-road, greeting each vehicle with long Bren bursts until it ran off the road and overturned, often in flames.

Gradually calm settled on the town. It was ours. We had taken fifty vehicles, including trucks and lorries loaded with loot, clothes, chocolate, and even British Red Cross cigarettes which must have been stolen from P.O.W. supplies. We had about seventy prisoners, some of whom spoke excellent English. Their attitude towards the war was that Britain and Germany should join together and wipe out Russia and Italy. They detested the Italians, blaming those in Termoli for their capture that morning. With great tact, they added that they considered it a great honour to be taken prisoner by Commando troops. Some of the men from No. 3 Commando recognised Germans who had been their captors in the Commando Bridge Battle. There were animated conversations, each side relating their experiences since that battle. The tables had been turned but the atmosphere was most friendly. We were able to repay the good treatment which the 4th German Parachute Brigade had given to our men who had been taken in Sicily.

After the fighting, I withdrew 40 Commando and the Special Raiding Squadron into Termoli to rest and refit. That left the perimeter seriously undermanned, but this was a calculated gamble on my part as these men had had only one decent night's sleep in the better part of a week, and I wanted them in tip-top shape in case they were needed. No. 3 Commando was left on outpost duty north of the town. Later that day the first Eighth Army troops began to arrive.

Arthur Komrower, who had rejoined us after recovering from his Vaagso injury, was commanding No. 3 Commando. I said to him:

"If it's all quiet tomorrow, I'll relieve you and send you straight back to Bari."

I thought No. 3 Commando had had enough by this time. The landing craft were still lying off Termoli, so I had the transport to send troops back if I wanted to.

Allan Peile secured for our Commando Brigade Headquarters the best house in the town, a big stucco villa overlooking the harbour. The house had belonged to a notorious Fascist, who had left with his wife on our approach. The butler, who was in charge, was typical of his English counterpart, of medium height and distinguished appearance, about fifty years old. He was most obstructive and had locked up all the best rooms. I told Allan to lock him up in the cellar till his mood changed.

On the Termoli operation we had taken with us a team of surgeons. Their role was to operate on the spot, saving men a long journey before they could be attended to. The surgeons took over the Termoli hospital and started immediate treatment on the casualties. Their devotion to duty was, I thought, admirable. I don't like the smell of hospitals and avoid entering them if I can, but I watched these surgeons at work with pride. However, a senior medical officer, a full colonel, who therefore outranked me, turned up at ten o'clock in the evening of the 3rd October and proceeded to lecture me on my lack of staff knowledge concerning medical problems. He was a typical old-line R.A.M.C. man who kept quoting King's Regulations. We hadn't acted through proper channels, he said. I was tired by this time and overwrought.

"You go to hell!" I shouted. "We know how to run our battles: when I want your advice I'll come and see you."

He didn't trouble us any more.

Allan Peile had got a beautiful bedroom ready for me and I was thankful to retire there.

The next day, the 4th October, began quietly. More supporting troops arrived with anti-aircraft and anti-tank guns.

The inhabitants had begun to show signs of being troublesome, however, and there was a great deal of civilian sniping. A patrol of 40 Commando on anti-sniping duties saw a man leave a house and throw a grenade at a gun position. I estimated the time between the man committing this offence and his execution to have been half a second. The incidents continued. Accordingly, I had the entire male population assembled in the town square and spread rumours of a mass execution. They went home in a more co-operative frame of mind. The sniping stopped.

That morning I spoke over the telephone, through an interpreter, to the Mayor of Guglionesi, a neighbouring town. Although the wire passed through the German lines it had not been cut.

"There are hundreds of German tanks here," the Mayor said.

I had other information from our Eighth Army Intelligence.

"Don't talk such bloody nonsense," I told him. "There are no tanks nearer than Rome."

I was aware from past experience that news of this sort was most unreliable at any rate.

A tall, slender, distinguished-looking Pole, with greying hair, appeared during the morning. He told me that he was a high-ranking diplomat, introduced me to his twelve-year-old son, and invited me to luncheon in an excellent restaurant. As we sipped our brandies, John Pooley rushed in.

"Colonel!" he said urgently. "There are dozens of tanks coming over the hill."

"If there are, John, don't shout about it," I replied. "But I don't think it can be true."

"Well, come out and see for yourself."

I went out on to the balcony. I saw at least fifteen German tanks nosing over a hilltop about two miles from where I stood.

"You're right," I said to Pooley. "Come inside and join us in a brandy."

I was not as unconcerned as I sounded. It just happened that we had no defence role at the moment, but were in reserve. At any rate, the Germans did not at this time commit their armour.

General Dempsey came up to see us that evening. I met him at the pontoon bridge which the Royal Engineers had strung across the Biferno River, replacing the original one which the Germans had demolished. Before this battle the General had been complaining that he was sick of seeing only Italian prisoners. Just then the very smart German Garrison Commander passed on his way back to captivity.

"There's a German for you, sir," I said.

"A real Hun!" the General commented, full of good humour.

Next morning I awoke early. I was shaving at 6 a.m. in my beautiful bathroom, when a dozen low-flying Messerschmitts came over, shooting and bombing. This was unusual, as the Germans were short of aircraft in Italy just then. Just after they had gone it began to rain heavily. I was suddenly acutely aware of impending danger. I had an idea that we were in for a strong German counter-attack. Added to that, there was the danger of rain flooding our temporary bridge away. This would cut us off from major reinforcements. I sent Allan Peile off to warn 40 Commando and the Special Raiding Squadron to stand to, and to caution all the other units in the town. Later I called round to warn the senior officer commanding these units.

"Don't exaggerate, Colonel," I was told by him. "We have things well in hand."

I shrugged and left. At least I could get on with our own defences. I sent Lofty King and two men to occupy an observation post on top of the town's principal hotel.

I also sent a message to Arthur Komrower to say that he would have to hold on with No. 3 Commando where he was. Brian Franks got 40 Commando and the Special Raiding Squadron into position to form a tight perimeter round the town and they at once dug themselves in.

Italian rivers fill with extraordinary speed in heavy rainstorms. Our bridge was swept away in a couple of hours. By eight o'clock that morning the enemy artillery barrage began, consisting of all the Divisional Artillery of the 16th Panzer Division, with a few heavy guns attached. During the night, a German artillery observer had managed to infiltrate through our lines into the town—it was a big perimeter with many

gaps in it—and had set up an observation post with a commanding view. He brought fire on a unit of our troops moving
out to the perimeter, landing a direct hit on one truck and
killing those in it.

His next target was our headquarters, which he must have
located from the wireless aerials. I was conferring with Brian
Franks in my office. An eighty-eight mm. shell burst in the
adjacent room where some of my staff were busy.

"We'd better have a look," I said to Brian. "Let's hope
they're all right." Brian went in first.

"My God," he said, "they're not!"

Tim Leese, who had insisted on coming back after losing an
eye in the Commando Bridge Battle two months before, was
dead. Allan Peile had been blown out of the window. He was
hanging from the sill with a serious concussion, clinging there
instinctively, not knowing, until we pulled him in, if he were
dead or alive. We moved our office to the ground floor, choosing
the room with the strongest walls. The barrage continued.

The streets of Termoli were, by this time, strewn with broken
glass and rubble. Great, jagged holes gaped in the buildings.
One shell dropped in a roadway and killed four soldiers
walking along the pavement. There were many fires, including
several blazing haystacks, on the edges of the town. As night
fell, they became bright, unwelcome beacons. The battle was
not now going in our favour.

Peter Young arrived from hospital. He was suffering from
malaria and jaundice and wasn't fit to take over No. 3 Commando, so he stopped in my headquarters to help me.

"How's it going?" he asked.

"If Billy Hill, the bookmaker, was here he'd be laying
evens," I told him.

The Commando troops, well dug-in, had not given an inch
but the newly-arrived supporting units, tired from their
hurried march and in badly-prepared positions, sometimes
could not hold the enemy. By all the accepted rules the Germans had won the battle, and many of the supporting units
started to fall back. They had been beaten by a good enemy
with greatly superior fire power. I had to threaten many
officers and men—none of them ours—with shooting. Most

of them pulled themselves together. Our men refused to be
beaten and I knew that if only I could get the supporting
units to hold on, we should win the battle.

The same senior officer who had pooh-poohed my warning
of danger, fussed and nagged a great deal. Finally, he left
me.

"I'm off to die at the head of my troops," he said, dramatically.

"I hope to God you do," I retorted, almost meaning it.

He made off down the road, heading into his first action.
He did quite well later on.

Confusion filled that day. With the pontoon bridge swept
away, we were completely cut off from reinforcements. Things
looked bad. Jerry had a complete Panzer division and supporting troops and tanks against, on our side, one infantry
brigade and our Commando Brigade which was far from
being at full strength. We were outnumbered three to two
by the enemy. His supply lines were intact. Ours were non-
existent.

The Royal Engineers rebuilding the bridge performed an
epic feat. The Germans realised the significance of its recon-
struction and showered shells on the sappers, who were hard
at work over the roaring river. They completed the bridge by
nightfall. Then our tanks crossed in strength and the tide of
the battle began to swing in our favour. The weather also
changed, and we were able to get heavy air support. I now
knew that we were sure to win, but that it might take a little
time.

We had not yet been able to locate the German artillery
observer who had crept into the town. Movement of troops
and vehicles, even a party of two or three men, was always a
challenge to him and a danger to us. We cursed him, but could
not find him. I sent a party out to search for him at noon.
Finally, at five, they pinpointed his location to a church tower.
They crawled up the tower.

"Come down—surrender!" my men called.

The German answered with a shot from his revolver and
scurried up on to the roof. Now we sprayed the roof with
Bren gun fire, and, crawling up a minute or two later found
him there, sprawled dead beside his radio set. He was a tough

and brave man and, while he lived, a great threat to us in Termoli.

The fighting raged. No. 3 Commando, still out in front, were giving, during this German counter-attack, what was probably their finest performance of the war. Hammered by tanks, pounded by guns, attacked by infantry, and left exposed and bleeding on their left flank by the retreat of another unit, they did not budge from their positions. I sent them a message that I would get them out of Termoli that night. Roy Farran was acting as Liaison Officer for the Special Raiding Squadron. He was quiet and efficient, having every quality needed by a young officer. The Special Raiding Squadron and No. 40 Commando had also held on to every yard of their positions.

George Herbert who had come into my headquarters as Liaison Officer, spent that night with us. About 4 a.m. he lay down on the floor for a sleep and nestled close to an animal which he took to be a dog, cuddling it for warmth. In the cold light of dawn the dog turned out to be a pig.

"This damn, bloody, ——, ——!" George roared, unprintably furious. I think, however, the pig was very pleased. He had had a warm and comfy night.

The butler who had earlier been confined to the cellar was released from time to time to attend to my headquarters officers and men. He was in a much chastened mood, and produced hitherto undivulged stores of food and wine. We had kept the house clean and tidy throughout the battle. There was never any excitement, shouting or confusion in Commando Brigade Headquarters. I think that during the Termoli battle, all our Headquarters staff, whether sweeping the floor, controlling the battle, or dying, did their job well.

That day there was a terrific finale to the battle. Every gun we had, every mortar, tank, aeroplane and man combined to devastate the Germans. The enemy wisely cleared off in the face of such overwhelming fire power. At last I had a chance to look round. I found that my beautiful Horsch, left behind so kindly by General Heydrich, had been utterly destroyed by a shell outside our headquarters villa. Gears, wheels, upholstery, broken windows were scattered over the street like the parts of a dismantled clock. I tried to console myself with the thought that I was undoubtedly lucky not to have been in the vehicle at the time it was hit. This was the shortest period I ever owned a car.

Before we left Termoli, Monty came to pay us a visit. I told him that my men had deserved a rest.

"Take them away to Bari for a good holiday," the General said brightly. "There's plenty of everything down there."

This was the man who was supposed to be so austere, to disapprove of all frivolity. Monty was delighted that we had secured and held Termoli for him. The Commando Brigade's action had helped the Eighth Army forward, and had saved him from having to fight for the line of the Biferno River. It had also secured a useful harbour next to the front line where men and supplies could be landed. It had been a very near thing.

The flotilla of landing craft had been lying off Termoli throughout the battle, where they had been continually dive-bombed and shelled. Their Commander had thought, not without reason, that he might have to evacuate us. The troops left in the landing craft for Bari and Molfetta, where they were all able to have a good rest.

For the next few days I was restless and uneasy. As I had discovered before, it took me at least a week to unwind after a hard battle. Just when I was feeling fit again for anything I had a signal which quickened my pulse. It ordered me to return to Britain with No. 3 Commando. I knew this meant we were to participate in the D-Day landings.

CHAPTER XII

PLANNING FOR D-DAY

WHEN I reached Britain, on the 30th October, 1943, there were changes afoot in the Commando organisation. Until then there had been only one Royal Marine Commando, the all-volunteer No. 40 which had taken part at Dieppe and Termoli. Now other Marine Commandos, a mixture of volunteers and conscripts, were being formed. I was dead against the idea.

Perhaps I was prejudiced. I was proud of the volunteer tradition of the Commandos. More important, I was convinced, in spite of Mountbatten whose idea this was, that units of conscripted marines could not be expected to maintain the high Commando standards.

The war had now reached a stage where raiding was nearly finished with. The Commando role was to land and hold on, as we had done at Termoli. There might still be small-scale reconnaissance raids, but there would be no more Vaagso's or Dieppe's. With this in view, the Commandos had been reorganised into four self-contained brigades, one to remain in Italy, one to go to the Far East, and two to operate in north-west Europe. To control these four brigades, Commando Group Headquarters was set up. General Robert Sturges, Royal Marines, was in command of Commando Group, and I was appointed as his Deputy Commander and was promoted to brigadier.

Commando Group Headquarters was at Pinner. I went down there to meet General Sturges. He was a battle-experienced Royal Marine officer, full of fun. He knew how to work and how to play.

"Your job will be to look after the interests of the army Commandos," Bob Sturges said to me. "Also, I want you to run all the planning for D-Day. You ought to know how to do that."

COMMANDO

I could see it was a happy, well-run headquarters. After luncheon Bob Sturges said:

"You look a bit tired. You had better have some leave."

He was quite right. I needed leave after our strenuous time in Italy.

When I got back to Pinner I decided to visit both the brigades which were going to operate on D-Day. I found that the First Commando Brigade, commanded by Lord Lovat, was in a highly efficient state. He had in his brigade Nos. 4 and 6 Army Commandos, both experienced, well-trained units. No. 3 Commando was on its way back to join him. The fourth unit was No. 45 Royal Marine Commando. This was a recently raised unit and had a long way to go to catch up with the army Commandos, but I thought under Lord Lovat, and in such good company, they would be sure to make the grade. The Fourth Commando Brigade, also due to operate on D-Day, consisted of Nos. 46, 47 and 48 Royal Marine Commandos, all recently formed. Brigadier Jumbo Leicester was the Brigade Commander. He realised that he had a very big job on hand to get his units ready. I liked him at once, and thought he would overcome the difficulties. No. 41 Royal Marine Commando was due home from Italy to complete the Brigade.

Bob Sturges told me to go to the Royal Marine Headquarter Office in London, to tell them about the activities of the Royal Marine Commandos in Sicily and Italy.

"You may find them a bit sticky," he said.

I decided to take the opportunity of impressing on them the necessity of sending really good men to their new Commandos. Up to this time they had sent a mixture. I was shown in to see a very senior Royal Marine officer. I told him how well No. 40 Commando had done it Italy, and said:

"This was largely due to the fact that they were a volunteer unit."

He took offence at this and said: "There's no need for volunteering with us."

I asked him to get down to basic facts and to realise that only picked men were good enough. Sometimes as much as one quarter of the drafts sent to us from Royal Marine establishments had been rejected by our Commando Depot. I was genuinely worried that we would have a failure on D-Day unless things improved. After this talk, the officers and men sent to us were of a more suitable type.

The Commando reputation now stood very high and we had every help from the War Office, which had been completely converted to our cause. Every general operating on D-Day wanted to have Commandos with him. They thought it a very handy thing to have units who would take on the tough jobs and be certain to bring them off. This trust placed in the Commandos made it all the more important that both the army and Marine Commandos should be in a highly efficient state. I was continually visiting units, encouraging them and helping them with their training. The officers and men in the new Royal Marine Commandos were keen to learn and keen to fight. It was their headquarters who had at first let them down in sending them bad material. Gradually we got things sorted out and got the right officers and men.

In late November while dancing at the "400 Club" at about 2 a.m. I received a message that I was to go the next day to luncheon at Chequers with Mr. Churchill. The procedure was that a large car would pick me up at my hotel and I was then to call at the Dorchester to pick up Miss Mary Churchill and take her down with me. I am very susceptible to hiccoughs and on the day in question had a terrible and prolonged attack. Miss Churchill was very kind in the car going down and kept telling me all would be well; nevertheless I went into luncheon in a state of great fear.

I sat next to Mr. Churchill, who was not at first in a good mood as he had been transacting some troublesome business. He was soon himself again, however, and the luncheon and the conversation were so good that I never gave the hiccoughs another thought. I finished up with one of the famous cigars, and after luncheon had half-an-hour alone with Mr. Churchill. He wanted to know the soldiers' opinion of Monty and Dempsey, whose appointments for D-Day had not at that time been announced. I do not suggest that my opinion had any effect on these appointments, but I certainly did not do these famous generals any harm in what I said. When it was time for me to go, Mr. Churchill took me out to the car, told the chauffeur to drive carefully, shook me by the hand and said:

"I am proud to have met you."

In November I also started studying the D-Day planning. The essential factors were that a port capable of handling large ships should be included in the area, that the sea voyage should be as short as possible, and that fighter aircraft should with ease be able to cover operations in France from British bases. It was soon agreed that the Normandy area would be best and the Caen area was finally chosen as the best place of lodgement. It was not powerfully defended, the fields could easily be turned into airstrips and the terrain afforded the Germans little opportunity for large panzer assaults. Plans for the opening phases up to the capture of Cherbourg, and developments after its capture, had to be considered, also the selection of suitable beaches. The timing of the assault was also of great importance. All these factors had to be investigated during this planning period, and from one great overall scheme the Commandos' role would emerge and be detailed at Commando Group Headquarters.

It was my job to co-ordinate and supervise the planning as it affected the Commandos. I could see plenty of work for them, but decided that there was time enough to fit in their employment when the plans became a little more advanced. I was continually studying the maps and photographs and was quite sure the initial landing would be safely made. At the same time I was a bit apprehensive about what might happen in the few days after landing. The happy and confident attitude of the Eighth Army was missing among the planners. There were continual rumours that Monty and Dempsey were going to take over. I longed for this to happen and I knew the plan would be improved out of all recognition after they had studied it.

For relaxation during this pre-invasion period, I took to visiting the dog tracks occasionally. Jack Solomons, the boxing promoter, whom I knew quite well, heard of this and sent me a message that if I came to Catford one Saturday afternoon,

he would run a dog which was sure to win. Jack seemed
to have a soft spot for Commando soldiers. I went down to
Catford with two of my friends. When we arrived Solomons
cautioned us not to approach the bookmakers.

"I want to get a good price in this race," he whispered.

We gave the money to his man to place for us. I was so
sure that this was a good tip that I invested £60 on the dog,
all I could scrape up.

The traps flew open, and in the first few seconds Jack's dog
was left twenty lengths behind. I groaned, turning away in
disgust, certain I had lost my bet. A moment later, hearing
a roar from the crowd, I looked back. The dog was rapidly
making ground. I yelled encouragement and Jack helped me.
In the last few feet our dog just managed to win by a short
head. The odds were six to four and I knew I would not be
short of funds for a while. I thanked Solomons, sighing heavily.

"That shook me, Jack!" I added.

"It shook *you*?" he retorted, grinning broadly. "What do
you think it did to me?"

I believe he had put a great deal more on the dog than I had.

In December I went up to our Commando Depot at Achnacarry. Colonel Charles Vaughan was passing all the newly
formed Royal Marine Commandos through a rigorous course
of training. Men were worked to the limit in order that their
failings should be discovered in training and not in the battle.
Life was very tough at Achnacarry, but Colonel Vaughan's
training produced a complete transformation, and the new
Royal Marine Commandos were beginning to take shape.
Charles Vaughan asked me to talk to the men up there. I
told them of our experiences in Sicily and Italy and ended
by saying:

"If you learn everything you are taught here, your success
on D-Day will be certain."

I felt this to be true and was beginning to feel a good deal
happier about D-Day. There was still an ample flow of good
men for the army Commandos. I knew they would do their
stuff. I told Charles to keep a good selection for No. 3 Commando, for they needed nearly two hundred replacements.

In January, 1944, Monty and Dempsey arrived home to

take over the 21st Army Group and the 2nd Army respectively. Immediately, the whole atmosphere lightened. The D-Day plan was improved as I had anticipated. The slight gloom lifted. The difficulties of the West Wall were no longer regarded as insuperable. General Dempsey said to me:

"I want you to form a small Commando Headquarters to come with me and look after everything concerning the Commandos. You can live in my personal mess."

A few days later No. 3 Commando arrived back at Liverpool after a delayed journey. I went up with Shimi Lovat, their new Brigade Commander, to meet them. Before leaving London I told Roy Westley, who had come on to England ahead of the Commando to collect pay and clothing coupons. He collected six thousand pounds and three thousand clothing coupons. Shimi, Roy and I met and had dinner in London before catching the night train to Liverpool. We had a considerable party. Suddenly, I looked at my watch and found the train was due to leave in twenty minutes. We rushed out and hailed a taxi. Half-way to Euston I asked Roy if he had the money. He had left it behind in the restaurant. We quickly hailed another taxi and sent Roy back. He found the money and the coupons in the restaurant where he had left them. He caught the train as it was pulling out.

No. 3 Commando arrived, delighted to be met and looked after. I gave a party for most of the officers in the Adelphi Hotel. I remember John Pooley saying to me:

"This is the happiest evening of my life."

Next day they went on leave, and in a fortnight's time they were back at Worthing where they met their new recruits from Achnacarry. The same week Charlie Head and Charlesworth arrived back from hospital in Egypt. They both looked very ill, but begged to be allowed to join the small headquarters which I was to take to Normandy.

Monty soon developed the D-Day plans and gave the master touch to everything. He decided to extend the front a good deal and to use the beaches from Ouistream to Coursueilles. This meant that a large area on the left of the front had to be secured, including some high ground to the east of the River Orne. It was decided that this should be a task for an airborne

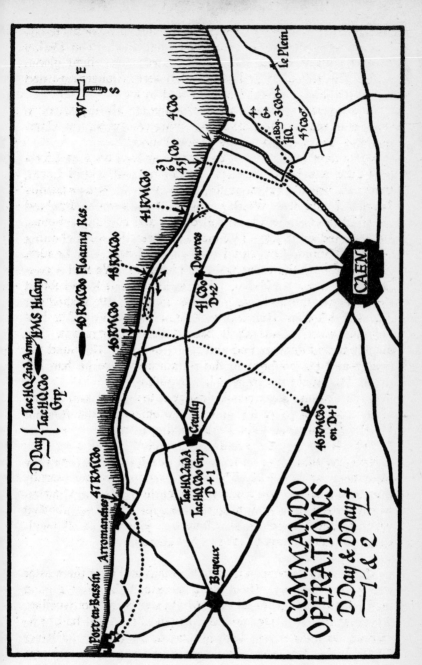

COMMANDO OPERATIONS
D Day & D Day +
1 & 2

D Day { Tac HQ 2nd Army
       { Tac HQ Cdo Grp.

━━━ HMS AstGry

━━━ 46 RM Cdo Floating Res.

W E N S

Le Plein

4 Cdo

3 Cdo
6
45

41 RM Cdo

48 RM Cdo

46 RM Cdo

47 RM Cdo

Port-en-Bessin
Arromanches

4 B.9 3 Cdo
H.Q.
4,5 Cdo

Douvres

41 Cdo
D+2

CAEN

Creully

Tac HQ 2nd A
Tac HQ Cdo Grp
D+1

Bayeux

46 RM Cdo
on D+1

division supported by the First Commando Brigade. The First Commando Brigade was to land at Ouistream, fight their way through five miles of uncleared country to the Orne bridges, cross the River Orne, and link up with the airborne troops. They were then to dig in and hold on until relieved. Many people said to me in the early stages that the plan was fantastic and impossible. There is no doubt that an ordinary brigade would never have reached the Orne bridges in time, let alone join up with an airborne division and hold on to their position. However, I knew that Lord Lovat's Brigade was capable of doing the job.

"Will it be all right?" General Dempsey asked me.

"Yes," I said. "Given a good landing, they are sure to get there. Try not to leave them out there on their own too long."

No. 4 Commando Brigade were to be used for work which was equally hazardous but not so spectacular. They were to operate as individual Commandos against key points in Hitler's West Wall. Having captured these key points, they were to join up as a brigade and were to join No. 1 Commando Brigade on the left flank. I thought this was exactly the right thing for them. They would get their battle experience in the initial assault, and then would come up to support the 1st Brigade. I was happy and confident about the whole thing.

No. 3 Commando settled in at Worthing under Peter Young and began hard training. I soon found that my own feelings against conscripted Marine Commandos were almost universally shared by army Commando officers and other ranks.

Lofty King was Provost Sergeant at Worthing. He was among those who felt most strongly that the new men did not merit the Commando label. In fact, he soon broadcast a ruling.

"No bloody marine is to come into this town!" he decreed.

Only one ever tried. One evening not long after his laying down of that law, Lofty went into his favourite public house. He stiffened when he saw a marine there, a young man, pink-cheeked and healthy.

"Enjoying yourself, sonny?" Lofty said, with false good humour.

"Yes, Sergeant." Obviously the Marine had heard neither of Lofty nor his ruling.

"Well, have a pint of beer," Lofty said.

The marine drank up.

"Now then," Lofty said, "come outside. I've got something to say to you."

What Lofty had to say was mostly with his fists. In a few minutes he was looking down at the prostrate form.

"Now, get the hell out of Worthing," he ordered. "Tell your marine friends how we feel about them."

Of course this attitude was not exactly a healthy one for inter-unit relations. In spite of my own feelings I soon found that my most important task was to promote amity between army and Marine Commandos. I told Peter Young and Lofty that this sort of thing had got to stop. At first I was misunderstood by the army Commandos, who thought I had gone over to the cause of the marines, but gradually the feeling of resentment died down.

During this period of readying ourselves for the great assault against the Continent, I was determined that those Commandos who had in previous operations taken the most consistent risks should be placed in safer employment. None would hear of it, but, by issuing a direct order, I had George Herbert, John Pooley and Brian Butler posted to our depot at Achnacarry. There, I felt with relief, they would miss the Normandy landings. Johnny Dowling and Lofty King, however, managed to persuade me. They remained with No. 3 Commando throughout. During the next few weeks I had a stream of messages from the three at Achnacarry, each more full of misery than the last. They liked the training, they said, but it was not the same as being in No. 3. Finally I weakened with them too. Happily back to the unit came Herbert, Pooley and Butler.

In February I formed the small headquarters which was to operate in Normandy. I chose Charlie Head, Allan Peile, Charlesworth, and one or two others. I wanted experienced men. We set up a planning headquarters in Ashley Gardens, Victoria; it was part of General Dempsey's 2nd Army Headquarters. There we started to study the D-Day landings in detail. Life in the Mediterranean had been nearly all work and no play, and planning in the West End of London was highly appreciated by myself and my small staff. There followed a period of working hard all day, and playing hard most of the night, but our duties were never neglected. Charlie and Allan Peile were continually making useful suggestions which I passed on to the brigade commanders. We met wonderful new friends and life in general was exactly right.

In 1927, when I went up to London for my army examination, I visited the London Pavilion where I saw and heard Edythe Baker playing "My Heart Stood Still" and "The Birth of the Blues" on an enormous white piano. I thought this the greatest thing I had experienced, and was still of the same opinion in 1944. One evening in March, Charlie and I were being put up in a flat in South Audley Street and the bathroom accommodation was somewhat overtaxed. Our hostess said that she would get the use of the bathroom in the flat above, this being Edythe Baker's flat. Edythe Baker is highly domesticated, and she personally cleaned out the bath, ran it and put in the bath salts. As I lay in the bath I could hear "My Heart Stood Still" being played on the piano. The greatest bath of all time? Of course it was. We all felt that we had better enjoy ourselves while we could.

The planning went on smoothly. Charlie and Allan Peile had the full confidence of Shimi Lovat and Jumbo Leicester who were commanding our brigades. Shimi and Jumbo were always willing to listen to their suggestions. I had one severe set-to with Shimi Lovat. He was anxious that No. 4 Commando should attack a battery at Houlgate, some miles to the east of Ouistream. This battery commanded part of the D-Day anchorage. No. 4 Commando could certainly have taken and destroyed the battery, but would then have been faced with the task of making their way back to our lines through miles of German-held territory.

"That's just what we've been training for all the time you were away in the Mediterranean," said Shimi.

I was dead against risking the elimination of No. 4 Commando on the first day of the battle. I said:

"Maybe the R.A.F. will look after the battery."

This was the only point on which we couldn't agree. General

Dempsey gave me the casting vote and the R.A.F. took on the job. Jumbo Leicester, commanding No. 4 Brigade, at first seemed rather over-cautious and seemed to weigh the difficulties too heavily. I soon found that it was only his thorough method of approaching things. His Marine Commandos were coming on fast and I felt they would be capable of doing their job.

In the Mediterranean I had promised the officers of No. 3 Commando a real party on their return to England, "the greatest party of all time." Charlie Head kept saying to me:

"What about that party? The boys are expecting it."

"All right," I said. "You go ahead and organise it."

I learnt that Admiral Sir Geoffrey Layton had three or four dozen bottles of champagne to sell, so I sent Charlie Head down to his home with instructions to strike the hardest possible bargain. Charlesworth, a Lancashire man, was sent on a week's leave with orders to tour the North Country and produce the necessary food. After three days he sent me a telegram which read, "So far have only secured seventeen chickens." Jack Solomons arranged to provide four hundred oysters and forty lobsters. We hired a club near Piccadilly for the evening. None of the officers were allowed to bring their girl friends; we entrusted this important matter to Lady Queensberry and Mrs. Bob Laycock, asking them each to bring the ten loveliest girls they could find. Edythe Baker agreed to play "My Heart Stood Still" and "Birth of the Blues."

This somewhat curious mixture produced a magnificent party. The girls included Margaret Sweeney, Penelope Dudley Ward, Elizabeth Allen, Mary Churchill, Polly Peabody, Loelia, Duchess of Westminster, together with many others of the same calibre. It was a little quiet to start with, but the champagne soon did its work and with the good company and a good band I was able to relax. Ted Greeno and Nat Thorpe from Scotland Yard were there, also William Hill, the celebrated bookmaker. On the roof we had two of our signallers, connected by telephone to the club, spotting for air raids. Alternative accommodation in the basement had been arranged for the party in the event of a serious raid. A fleet of cars had been available throughout the evening for transport.

Towards the end of the evening, William Hill asked Charlie Head who was going to pay for everything. Charlie told him a very sad story about the impecunious Brigadier breaking himself in order to redeem his promise of a party. Billy Hill summoned the proprietor of the club and asked him how much all this would cost. Within a couple of minutes Billy wrote out a cheque for £200. The officers subscribed £5 each and I paid the balance, which was not a great deal. I wanted these officers to have the best of everything, for they certainly deserved it. Very shortly they were to take part in another hazardous operation.

We were most anxious to get a good selection of padres for the forthcoming operations in Europe. General Sturges obtained an excellent naval padre called John Armstrong and told him to select a really good lot of junior padres to act with units. It was known that I had been a severe critic of some of our early padres. In January, 1944, John Armstrong asked me to address these men as to their duties. I was somewhat shy about this but eventually agreed. We called them all to Group Headquarters and I gave them a long talk. I stressed the matter of cheerfulness and confidence in the outcome of the battle. I had noticed that the attitude of the padre in battle spread very quickly to the men. I told them that their attitude of confidence must start from that day and that they must be the friends and advisors of the soldiers. I went on to say that they must regard themselves as being highly privileged to accompany into battle the great fighting men of the units they were with. They were not to try and alter the ways of the men, certain of whom would no doubt go on gambling, drinking and chasing the girls. The most important thing for them was sincerity. One good church parade a month was enough, with a short, topical sermon, preferably stressing the activities of St. Paul, whom I always regarded as the patron saint of the Commandos. I told them that if any man said things were tough or depressing the padre must pull him up sharp. They must be able to help with medical work and intelligence work. I think the talk went down well and we were well served in north-west Europe by our ecclesiastical helpers.

In April, 1944, Charlie Head again was sent to hospital. His leg wound had not healed satisfactorily. Charlie was a major now, a liaison officer for Commando Group, but he still acted largely as my personal assistant. I received a sad letter from him in hospital. He was afraid he was not going to be able to come with my headquarters to Normandy; yet he could not bear to be left out of the show.

"In view of the fact that I'm a very powerful swimmer," Charlie wrote, "I feel I ought to be used in the invasion as a frogman to deal with underwater defences." He meant it.

He was determined to get to France whether on his feet or under water. I could tell that he was working himself into a state and visited him at once.

"If you can get out of hospital, Charlie," I promised, "you can forget about this frogman business. You can come with me."

"I'll get out," he said.

He knew that the one sure way of accomplishing this was to make a nuisance of himself. He proceeded to do this with remarkable thoroughness. Two days later, he was back at work.

Late in April, 1944, we moved Commando Group Headquarters so as to be nearer Southampton, our port of embarkation. Everything was ready, and commanding officers had received preliminary briefs from their brigade commanders. No information as to dates, times or places had been given, but the Commandos had enough to work on in order to rehearse their invasion roles.

General Dempsey arrived to inspect Lord Lovat's First Commando Brigade. Shimi Lovat decided that the inspection should be carried out mounted, as both General Dempsey and General Sturges were noted horsemen. When General Dempsey arrived, Shimi had three of his horses ready. The Generals and Lord Lovat mounted. The rest of us followed in jeeps. The three horsemen set off, and after a furlong General Dempsey's mount gave a tremendous buck, putting the General on the floor. I was horrified to see Shimi examining his beautifully bred horse for damage before asking the General if he was all right. We had a great day; General

Dempsey was in splendid spirits and everybody was delighted to be operating with him.

On the 2nd June, the First and Fourth Commando Brigades and my small headquarters which was to accompany them, moved into their concentration areas at Southampton. Charlie Head and I travelled round visiting all the Commandos. In the First Commando Brigade the troops were laughing and singing and the officers were confident and contented. Charlie and I had a wonderful reception from No. 3 Commando. All the old faces were there: Peter Young, Lofty King, Johnny Dowling, George Herbert, John Pooley, Brian Butler.

"It's nice to have you back with the unit, where you belong," George Herbert said.

It was good to *be* back, even if only for a short stay. When I left, it was with a feeling of sadness. I was sending them, for the first time, to do the job without me. I suppose this was the peculiar guilt of command. There would be men wounded and killed and I would not be taking the same assault chances as they did. Yet I had a feeling of contentment too; for here was the greatest combined operation of them all, and we had been the guinea pigs who had helped to make it possible. From now on, we were no longer on our own for independent sorties against the enemy. We were part of the big show.

No. 3 Commando were to land, with the rest of the First Commando Brigade, at La Breche to the west of Ouistream. They then had to advance four miles to the bridges over the River Orne. If the bridges had been destroyed, they were to ferry themselves over in rubber boats. They would continue the advance in a north-easterly direction, seizing the high ground near Le Plein. This was a task of no little magnitude, but I felt they would do it.

We went on to see the Fourth Commando Brigade. Here the atmosphere was different, serious determination taking the part of the exuberant spirits shown by the First Commando Brigade. The new Royal Marine Commandos were very serious-minded, but they had confidence in their ability to do their work. They were determined to show the army Commandos that Marine Commandos were fully capable of doing their stuff. They were never to attain the skill and finish of the army Commandos, but they had become good, steady units.

Final briefing was carried out in the concentration areas. Every man saw the models and photographs and knew exactly what he was expected to do. Charlie and I went back to our Headquarters and saw that our men were briefed as well.

On the last Saturday before D-Day, briefing had been completed. I was talking to Charlie and Shimi Lovat when Charlie said:

"There's racing at Ascot. Let's have a final day there."

When we got to the course I saw Fred Darling, who told me that his "Neola" would run well. It was common knowledge that D-Day was imminent as all leave had seen stopped and there were scarcely any soldiers on the course, except ourselves. William Hill seemed surprised to see us and gave Shimi and me preferential odds on "Neola," two to one on instead of three to one on, the ruling price. He thought he would lay us a favourable price before D-Day. Charlie Head laid ten pounds to five, and then, not being content with the price, approached Billy Hill and talked to him so persuasively that Billy laid *him* a further bet of five pounds to nothing in order to bring the odds for Charlie's total bet to evens. A little fellow in the crowd, who did not look exactly as if he were going on the D-Day operation, overheard the conversation and rushed forward, shouting at Billy:

"Even thousand, Bill."

"Who the —— hell do you think you are? Take three to one," was William Hill's reply.

"Neola" won by eight lengths, we felt it was a good omen.

On the evening of Sunday, the 4th June, I moved into General Dempsey's headquarters near Portsmouth, as the General wished me to travel with him on D-Day. He told me that the operation was postponed for a day, so I went to Highclere, near Newbury, where Lord Carnarvon had asked me to spend the week-end. I thought that the Highclere food and atmosphere would be a good prelude to the battle.

CHAPTER XIII

THE SECOND FRONT

I DROVE back from Highclere on the Monday, the 5th June, 1944, hoping that there would be no more postponements. I went to see General Dempsey.

"It's on this time," he said.

Everything had the calm and quiet atmosphere of the Eighth Army days. On the morning of D-Day I sailed with General Dempsey, Commander of the 2nd Army, in a destroyer. My job that day was to advise him about the Commando operations, and, in particular, to advise him as to the use of No. 46 Commando, which we had kept in floating reserve. We were ready to put No. 46 in at any place where the first landings might have failed.

At last the line of the French coast could be seen in the grey morning light. To the east, the hills behind Cobourg stood out clearly, but straight ahead where No. 3 Commando was to land, the coast was flat. Everywhere there were boats, from battleships to the smallest of landing craft. Then came the thunder of big guns as the navy began firing salvo after salvo at targets ashore.

As we neared the coast, signals came through on the radio saying that all the Commando landings had been safely accomplished. I wondered how No. 3 Commando was getting on, and wished I was with them. Peter Young's account vividly describes their experiences.

"During the afternoon of the 5th June, units left the camp by bus and were gradually concentrated on the coast near the anchorage at Warsash. To while away the time between arriving here and embarking, a football match was played against 6 Commando.

"No. 3 Commando embarked at 1700 hours, after which the craft moved out to an anchorage in Southampton Water. The

187

array of ships and craft of all descriptions which then became visible was truly impressive.

"At 2100 hours, sailing orders were received, the troops were mustered on deck and their destination made known. Shortly after this anchors were weighed and the fleet set sail. Troop cooks were soon busy preparing a gigantic meal from the plentiful supply of compo rations, the *pièce de resistance* being the tins of self-heating soups and cocoa. These might be included among the great inventions of the war. One merely applied a fuse to the wick on top of the tin and in literally less than a minute the contents were boiling.

"Once clear of the Isle of Wight the wind freshened considerably. All through the night and during the next morning the small craft pitched and rolled in an alarming manner and an increasing number of unhappy individuals were to be observed lining the rails. However, this made the cooks' task at breakfast unusually light and relieved the congestion below decks which had been acute.

"As the craft drew closer, further details became visible; small craft were battering their way through the heavy seas, ferrying troops ashore and returning to their parent ships. Spouts of water all around them indicated that the enemy were not idly looking on. Closer still, a line of battered, roofless buildings could be seen on the seafront, testimony to the accuracy of the pre-H-hour bombardment. A few tanks could be seen on the beach, their guns occasionally spouting flame. Their targets were invisible but this caused much speculation as to the degree of opposition the enemy were putting up.

"When about a thousand yards from the shore, the craft came under fire. Airbursts appeared overhead and shell splinters smacked into the water. Accounts at this time are varied. One man's impression was that the enemy were laying a curtain of fire along a line about two hundred yards from the beach.

" This enemy fire by now was far too accurate to be pleasant, and the small craft were rocked by the explosions from near misses while shell splinters rattled on the decks. Away to the left a tank landing craft was burning fiercely and the crew were seen scrambling off as the ammunition exploded. Three of the Commando's craft received direct hits from high-velocity shells.

No. 6 Troop's boat was badly holed and all the three-inch mortar ammunition exploded. The Troop sustained at least twenty casualties before the craft beached. Nevertheless, in view of the sustained and accurate enemy fire, overall casualties during the landing were much less than was expected.

"Most of the troops were still below decks during the run-in, but some were crouched behind the ramps, prepared to rush ashore as they were lowered.

"Corporal Jennings and Sergeant Osborne of No. 3 Troop could be seen sitting fully exposed in the stern, criticising each shot from the German battery and encouraging the enemy with such instructions as, 'Put your sights up, Jerry.' 'Down a little and give her more wind gauge,' as the shells came over and missed the craft. With each miss they cheered anew and offered the Germans further advice. As No. 3 Troop's landing craft beached, Johnny Dowling led the advance down the ramp. When he was half-way into the water a shell burst within a yard of him and he was wounded. He was evacuated to England the next day but was back in four weeks, as full of life as ever.

"Unfortunately the craft had grounded on a false beach some distance from the water's edge. Consequently the heavily-laden men, having plunged into about five feet of water, experienced some difficulty in reaching dry land. It was not altogether surprising, therefore, that a number of bicycles were lost in transit to the shore.

"The beach was negotiated without much difficulty in spite of wire and obstacles, and soon the Commando was being assembled under cover of the houses between the sand dunes and the road. It was a scene of confusion. Large numbers of troops were lying about in the sand dunes and very little appeared to be happening, although the enemy were maintaining sporadic mortar fire.

"After a check in the houses, lasting only a few minutes, 3 Commando moved off to the forming-up point, a large clump of bushes about a thousand yards inland. The route lay across flat, marshy ground, intersected by deep ditches. Patches of reeds afforded the only cover. Naturally, progress was slow, for men frequently floundered waist-deep in slime. The enemy were bringing down artillery fire but fortunately the soft nature of the ground greatly minimised its effect and casualties were few.

"Lieutenant Coweson, one of the section commanders, was severely wounded by a shell burst and his duties were taken over by Lofty King who commanded the section in an officer's capacity for the next three weeks. Lofty had been offered a commission in England, but preferred to remain as Troop Sergeant Major.

"On arrival at the forming-up point the Commando was found to be more or less intact, though 6 Troop was somewhat depleted and four officers had been wounded.

"The advance was now held up by mines, making wide deployment out of the question. The brigade was confined to one narrow track which had to be negotiated in single file. No. 6 Commando was already using this track, and, there being no alternative route, 3 Commando was held up at the forming-up point for some time, although the cycle troop had managed to push on.

"During their wait at the forming-up point, troops experienced for the first time the German multi-barrelled mortar, the Nebelwerfer, or 'Moaning Minnie' as it was aptly renamed. This weapon, like the JU 87B dive-bomber, was as effective against morale as it was in killing power. The characteristic moaning noise during the descent of the bomb was achieved by a special device fitted to the tail.

"At last the Commando was able to move off in single file, though progress was extremely slow, congestion ahead causing halts every few yards. The party passed through 45 Royal Marine Commando in Colleville, where things were found to be quiet, although some small arms fire was heard behind the houses. No difficulty was experienced along the road to St. Aubin d'Aquenay, but firing in that area caused the Commando to move through the village with more caution, making use of the cover afforded by the houses. At the far end of the village, troops belonging to 6 Commando were met bringing in German prisoners from the north-east.

"Beyond St. Aubin, the road was clear of troops and, as it led downhill to Benouville, much of this distance was covered at the double. Just before entering the village the party passed a section post manned by airborne troops who were obviously delighted to learn that the seaborne assault had been successful and that they were no longer isolated.

"On approaching the bridge over the Orne it was discovered to be under rifle fire from a large mansion on the west bank of the canal, eight hundred yards to the south. A number of dead Germans sprawling around and an abandoned glider within thirty yards of the road, were evidence of the airborne assault earlier in the day, while the fact that the bridges were intact was witness to the success of this operation.

"By crouching low and moving at the double the first bridge was crossed safely. Here a small party of 3 Troop was discovered. The men had dismounted from their bicycles and were taking cover under the low bank on the left of the road. They were ordered to mount and get across the far bridge as soon as possible. This was accomplished with the loss of one man killed.

"After crossing the bridge and contacting the headquarters of the airborne troops who had dropped the night before, it was found that the plan had to be modified. The airborne troops had dropped over a wider area than had been anticipated. No. 3 Commando would not, therefore, carry out their long advance to Cabourg, but would move instead to the area of Le Bas de Ranville, to protect Airborne Divisional Headquarters. No. 3 Troop under Roy Westley were detached, however, to capture Amfreville and Le Plein, villages which stood on the vital high ground overlooking a large part of the 2nd Army's landing area.

"Roy Westley and his troop advanced straight up the road. They had two miles to go. As they approached Le Plein the Germans opened fire from the village green. Roy became a casualty and Lieutenant Ponsford took over. Having reorganised the troop at the foot of the hill, Ponsford launched a second attack. This time a covered approach was chosen to the right of the road. The action was entirely successful and they entered the village, where they dug in and awaited reinforcements. Very soon the remainder of the Commando was relieved of their commitment at Le Bas de Ranville and were able to join up with 3 Troop. The whole of the Commando now came up and dug in. They were determined to hold on to the vital high ground around Le Plein. The remainder of the brigade then joined them. All units dug in and waited for the inevitable counter-attack. Their ambitious D-Day task had been accomplished."

I, myself, left the beach through a narrow gap in Hitler's iron wall. The first field I crossed held a dozen dead cows, legs pointing stiffly skyward. To our left a noisy battle was being waged as No. 48 Royal Marine Commando attacked one of the enemy's major strong points at Langrune. After suffering severe casualties, they reduced the strong point. Traffic was now moving freely through the beach exits, but the landing had been no walkover.

A military policeman drove me to our headquarters in an orchard near Creuilly, just across the road from General Dempsey's caravan. Charlie Head and Charlesworth had everything snug and comfortable. Charlie's leg was terribly lame: he had no business being there at all. He and Charlesworth, each wearing a bulky steel brace on an injured leg, had come ashore in an American landing craft. As they had gone down the ramp, an American captain, who had spotted their steel braces, shouted to Charlie:

"Say, Major, don't you and the corporal turn around when you get on the beach. If you do the Germans will think this is Dunkirk all over again."

Charlie and I went off to visit No. 1 Commando Brigade, commanded by Shimi Lovat. They were holding strongly on the ridge near Le Plein, against fierce, repeated counter-attacks. Both their flanks were open and they were under continual fire. Their flanks were not properly sealed for five days, until the build-up had given us enough troops to go round. They had a hell of a pounding in the meantime, but didn't budge an inch. Shimi was magnificent. Every time a mortar bomb burst I jumped a couple of feet while he stood rock still. I felt thoroughly ashamed.

A runner came rushing up from No. 4 Commando.

"We're being heavily counter-attacked, sir," he said to Lord Lovat.

"Tell 4 Commando to look after their own counter-attacks, and don't worry me until things get serious," Shimi said. We then resumed our conversation.

As Charlie and I left for our own headquarters, I said:
"You know, Charlie, I was damn windy then."

"Me, too," Charlie replied seriously. "Do you suppose
we're getting old?"

Of course, the real trouble was that we had not seen action
for a long time. It is more difficult to remain unmoved when
you come up from the back areas than it is for the man in the
front line. He, living in the constant atmosphere of danger,
has long since attuned his mind and body to the required pitch.

Charlie and I had a quick meal, picked up a Bren gun and
returned to Shimi with the offer that we should man a post for
the night. We were anxious to prove ourselves again.

"No, thank you," Shimi said, and meant it.

On the way back, I suddenly saw a huge German standing
by the roadside.

"Shoot him if he moves an inch!" I shouted to Charlie and
drove the jeep straight at him. The German's hands flew up.

"Kaput!" he said, with surprising meekness for such a giant.
He had been sent through our lines as a sniper, but as his heart
was not in the work he was delighted to be taken prisoner.

When we reached headquarters, "Lucy" McGovern, who
was then acting as my driver-batman, covered the German with
a pistol while we interrogated him. Our prisoner was wearing
a particularly fine lumber-jacket.

"You ought to have it," Charlie decided on my behalf.

He told McGovern to strip it from the German. In order
to do so, the driver unthinkingly handed his pistol to the
prisoner. The situation was ludicrous: a German prisoner with
a loaded revolver, faced by an unarmed British brigadier, a
major, and a private soldier. Fortunately this particular
prisoner had no guts at all. He surrendered his jacket. Then
he handed back the gun.

A battery was holding out at Merville near the coast. It
was shelling the shipping and had to be silenced. Nos. 4 and
5 Troops of 3 Commando, under John Pooley, were selected
for the operation.

The two troops approached the battery from the south,
following the road as far as Salenelles. Enemy mortars were
active during the approach march and 4 Troop lost two men.

Two jeeps were also destroyed in the village. From here the route to the battery was marked by hundreds of immense bomb craters. The final approach to the battery was across flat, completely open ground, rendering attack on the position an extremely hazardous operation.

No. 4 Troop approached frontally and took up a position in the hedgerow with the object of covering 5 Troop which, led by John Pooley, attacked from the east where there was a more covered approach.

Taking advantage of every scrap of cover afforded by ditches and hedgerows, 4 Troop edged forward to within three hundred yards of the battery, at the same time maintaining heavy small arms fire on the position. The battery had been fortified with typical German thoroughness. However, little could be seen of these fortifications except four large mounds rising twelve feet above the level of the field. These hid the gun emplacements—massive steel and concrete casemates, sunk deep into the ground and affording complete protection except from a direct hit by the heaviest bomb. Mines and wire added to the difficulties of an attacking force.

No. 4 Troop, having seen no sign of 5 Troop, sent a section to the left, but owing to the open nature of the ground on this side, the section could make little progress against the enemy small arms fire. At last, however, 5 Troop appeared from the left and charged the position with fixed bayonets. Although the defenders were few in number they fought fanatically and were very difficult to dislodge from the underground corridors and storerooms. Almost as soon as the troops reached the battery John Pooley was killed by a burst of fire from the entrance to one of the tunnels. The German responsible, and others who refused to surrender, were dealt with by grenades. The battery never fired again.

My daily routine was to visit both our brigades, finding out their needs, arranging for replacements, and dealing with their problems on the spot. They had heavy casualties just after landing, but most shocking to me personally was the news that Brian Butler, John Pooley and George Herbert were all killed early in the fight: John Pooley while leading an attack against the battery; Brian Butler, battling gallantly, on the very day he was promoted to the rank of Major; and George Herbert personally leading a determined and successful counter-attack. George was last seen advancing, roaring like a lion, firing a Bren from the hip, knocking the Germans right, left and centre, until, finally, he was himself shot through the heart. All three had been with me from the early days. They were my friends and advisers. It was because they had chanced their lives once too often in the past that I had posted all three to the safety of the depot. Why, I mourned, had I allowed them to argue their way back into battle? I wished with all my heart I had turned a deaf ear to their pleas.

The 4th Commando Brigade had carried out all their D-Day tasks successfully, and were ordered up to join the 1st Brigade and strengthen the position on the left. Before doing this, No. 41 Royal Marine Commando was detached to reduce a large underground radar station, which was holding out near Douvres, several miles behind the lines. Colonel Eric Palmer, the C.O., cheerfully undertook this task. Charlie Head organised tanks and artillery to support him. Charlie and I went to see his final attack. No enemy movement was to be seen above ground, but when we stood on a mound outside the perimeter, a heavy and accurate machine-gun fire was opened on us. The artillery put down smoke and No. 41 Commando came through the wire in perfect formation. They threw grenades down all the alleyways and slits which led to the underground passages and soon the Germans had had enough.

No. 46 Commando was also detached to make an attack with the 3rd British Division. Charlie and I went up to see this attack, which was opposed by two Tiger tanks. Colonel Campbell Hardy and No. 46 carried out a perfect attack and the Germans were driven off. I gave Campbell Hardy a bottle of gin and he told me he would keep it until evening. When evening came he shouted to his adjutant to bring the bottle. The adjutant hurried across the farmyard, slipped and fell and the precious bottle was broken. With No. 4 Commando Brigade established alongside No. 1 the position was secure and a period of static warfare set in.

One day during this heavy fighting Monty opened the door of his caravan at his headquarters near Creuilly, and was surprised to see a fully armed German soldier emerge from a wood about fifty yards distant. The German's only desire was to surrender, but the incident touched off fireworks amongst the security men. I was summoned by General Dempsey.

"There's been a serious breakdown in security in Monty's camp," he told me. "I want you to find a Commando troop to command a proper guard on him. But remember: Monty must know nothing about it. He hates having a lot of people around."

I selected a good troop from No. 41 Royal Marine Commando and told Charlie Head to look after the details. Charlie arranged for the troop to conceal themselves in the wood near Monty's caravan. He also had a hole dug under the caravan when its occupant was elsewhere and saw to it that it was camouflaged during the day. Charlie's scheme was for one of the marines to occupy this hole at night and from it to shoot any unauthorised person who might approach. A bearded marine duly took up his position at dusk on the first evening.

At about eleven o'clock that night Monty emerged from the caravan, flashing his torch. Keyed to fever pitch because of the importance of his assignment, the marine found this too much for his nerves to stand.

"Put that bloody light out!" he roared.

Monty hurried back to his caravan. He did not venture out again that night. In the morning, however, he demanded firmly that the entire troop return to their normal duties. That was the end of my special precautions.

On the 12th June, Lord Lovat was wounded while leading a counter-attack on the village of Breville in co-operation with the Airborne Division. The attack achieved its objective against very heavy odds, and artillery fire from our own side was brought down to help consolidate the position. A few shells fell short and a huge fragment from one of these cut deep into Lord Lovat's back. Though wounded himself, Colonel Derek Mills Roberts the next senior officer in the brigade, immediately took over and held on to the ground which had been gained. I knew this brigade remained in very capable hands. Derek was at once promoted to brigadier and continued to hold the command of the 1st Commando Brigade from that day until the brigade reached the Elbe.

The 1st Commando Brigade was most skilfully dug into the ground. Every man had his own foxhole, roofed over with strong timber, and so was reasonably safe except for a direct hit from a very large shell or bomb. The alarm system was most efficient and in a few seconds every man could be in a firing position if required. From these positions a murderous fire was opened against any counter-attack. The brigade had by now developed to a fine art the technique and discipline of holding their fire. They would wait until the Germans were about fifty yards away before opening up, when the entire attack would invariably be mown down. If you can achieve this once or twice nobody will come up for more. On the 14th June, I saw more than a hundred dead Germans directly in front of No. 3 Commando's position.

For the next few days patrolling and sniping continued on a bold scale and the enemy were given little rest. Six Germans who were hostile to the Hitler regime and who, in 1939, had come to England and enlisted in the British Army, were now attached to No. 3 Commando. For their own sakes these men were given British names and histories so that in the event of capture they might have a chance of survival. One of these men with the adopted name of Lawrence, continually went on solitary patrols under the German lines, listening to their conversations, and on three occasions he joined the Germans in their slit trenches and persuaded them to surrender. He tried this once too often and was captured, but his claim to British nationality was accepted and he was treated as a normal prisoner-of-war.

The 17th June was Derby Day and a bookmaker serving in General Dempsey's Headquarters set up his board and operated quite a straight and reasonable book. However, I was mindful of Charlesworths' experience at Suez and wishing to have a bet on Tehran I despatched Charlie Head to a neighbouring airstrip where the fighters landed after operational sorties to re-fuel before going on to England. Charlie's instructions were to give the slip with my bet and William Hill's telephone number on it to a responsible-looking pilot. Charlie told me that the man he approached was a Canadian fresh from a pretty hot sortie. Charlie told this pilot the true story of his eccentric Brigadier who insisted on getting his bet on and he further told him that the information was very good indeed so that the Canadians could all help themselves. Ocean Swell won the race and in due course I received my losing account from Billy Hill. Charlie and I kept well clear of the airstrip!

The old army-marine rivalry was by no means dead and I did my best to improve matters. When No. 4 Commando Brigade came up alongside 1 Brigade on the left flank I decided to give a party where army and marine officers might meet in a congenial atmosphere. I told Charlie Head to organise this party and he immediately purchased four geese and procured the necessary drinks. He obtained a French chef from our French Commando Troop who were fighting with No. 4 Commando. His name was Felix Maggi and he is now the head waiter of the Albany Club in Saville Row. After the first three geese had been killed the fourth looked at Charlie so appealingly that she was spared and accompanied us as a mascot all the way to Germany, where she was finally run over by a tank. The soldiers said she resembled McGovern the driver, and so she was named Lucy, which was his nickname. The party took place about three hundred yards from the front line on the boundary between the territories held by the two brigades. It was the greatest possible success. Nobody but myself was worrying at all about the possible enemy shelling and mortar fire but I must admit a great relief when this gathering of about sixty of our best officers was safely dispersed.

Every evening I had dinner with General Dempsey in his small personal mess; usually there were about six of us there. We talked about everything except the war. If there was business to be done I would go to his caravan afterwards. The General took the keenest interest in the Commandos and knew everything that went on. General Dempsey's A.D.C., Dawson, a son of the famous trainer, suggested to me that it would be a good thing if we could find a suitable horse so that the General could take an hour's exercise in the evenings. As usual I delegated my duties to Charlie Head, who returned in a couple of hours with a very fine ex-German charger. The General by now knew me pretty well and when I presented this horse to

him, had a slight suspicion that it had been extorted from some
unfortunate Frenchman. After repeated assurances from
Charlie and myself that the animal was indeed German, he
accepted the gift and was able to take what is surely the best
and most relaxing exercise in the world, an hour's quiet ride in
the evenings.

During this static period the Commandos directed their
energies into offensive patrolling, sniping and raiding. The
no-man's area of fields, woods and houses, between the lines
was completely dominated. Peter Young and No. 3 Commando
were established on the left flank of the 1st Commando Brigade
position, and Colonel Campbell Hardy and No. 46 Royal
Marine Commando were on the right flank of the 4th Commando Brigade position. These two brilliant and aggressive
Commanding Officers, therefore, held adjoining territories.
Both were very jealous of their rights and became furiously
indignant if the territories immediately in front of them were
trespassed on by patrols of the rival unit. No two Masters of
Foxhounds have ever been more jealous in maintaining their
territories. Later on they became the best of friends.

These actions kept the Germans in a state of constant tension
and kept the brigade fully informed as to the enemy dispositions.
During this period various booby traps and strange devices were
produced by both sides. No. 3 Commando made a frightening-
looking head of yellow gauze and wire painted with iodine
supplied by Ned Moore's first aid post: even in daylight it
looked alarming. Inside was fitted a light which could be
switched off and on from a position some distance from the
place where the head was sited. After dark the ghost head
was placed in front of our forward defence lines, usually half-
way up a tree, where it could be seen from the enemy lines.
It would be switched on for a few seconds at a time at irregular
intervals during the night. It was calculated that this appari-
tion glooming in the dark for a short while would cause a
certain amount of concern amongst the enemy and at least be
of some nuisance value if nothing else; at the same time it
caused quite a lot of amusement amongst our own troops at
a time when amusing incidents were getting scarcer every
day.

As the days wore on the strain of continuously manning front-line positions began to tell, and a very useful rest camp, where officers and men could relax and really rest for a couple of days, was established behind the lines. The majority of the men still lived in slit trenches, sleeping fully clothed and with their boots on. Their nights were almost always disturbed, even when not spent patrolling in no-man's-land and they were up before dawn every morning for "stand to."

Late in June I went to England to speed up the flow of rein-forcements. General Sturges came to France to run our small headquarters while I was away. All the marine officers thought that this would be the end of Charlie Head. They had seen him and Allan Peile fooling and enjoying themselves in England, and that when General Sturges came into close contact with him, he would be dismissed. They opened a selling sweep on the number of hours Charlie would survive after General Sturges took over. The most eagerly bid for times were zero, one and two hours. Anything over thirty-six hours was completely out. They did not understand that fooling and liquor formed no part of Charlie's life when he was on or near the battlefield. The General and Charlie were completely kindred spirits and became the greatest of friends.

I arranged the matter of the reinforcements and was back within a week. I felt out of it in England.

When we had visitors it was my invariable custom to include in our hospitality a trip to No. 1 Commando Brigade's lines for a little battle experience. The good soldiers loved this and the more timid ones hated it like hell. Each visitor was taken on a patrol, some of which were genuine, some bogus. The latter went out into no-man's-land all right, but not far enough to run into trouble. I remember having one young officer for tea. Then I told him I had arranged a patrol for his benefit. He turned pale as paper.

"My General wouldn't like me to be exposed to danger," he said.

This from a so-called soldier made me see flaming red.

"You'll go up and take what's coming to you," I roared, "and I hope they get you!"

The young officer soon agreed that a patrol was preferable to further blasting from me. I got on the telephone to Peter Young and told him to make this patrol a hot one. Then I relaxed and went off to have dinner with General Dempsey. After dinner I was surprised to find the young officer back from his patrol in the greatest of good humour. Later I asked Charlie Head what had happened.

"Nothing much," Charlie grinned. "Peter Young laid on one of his bogus patrols, a really fine one. He hid some men in the bushes with Bren guns. When the 'patrol' came along the men in ambush fired over their heads and most of the 'patrol' pretended to fall down dead."

The young officer guest, with Peter and a couple of others, had returned to our lines as the few "survivors." Charlie told me that this was the victim's first "battle experience." I felt certain he would not be so windy after that.

Two ladies became honorary members of our small headquarters. They were Cathleen Mann,. the artist, in private life Lady Queensberry, who had been commissioned by the magazines *Time* and *Life* to paint portraits of all the leading generals, and Polly Peabody from Boston, U.S.A., authoress of *Occupied Territory*, who was in search of material for a new book. They came and went as they liked and they lived exactly as we did, never causing any trouble. They were keen to have the usual battle experience and we arranged it in a modified form. They always liked visiting the front line.

We had at this time arranged a daily courier service to Main Commando Group Headquarters at Lavington Park, Petworth. The object was to keep in the closest touch with General Sturges, so as to ensure the immediate dispatch of reinforcements, stores and other necessary items, in order that no Commando should be kept waiting for anything it needed. On most days the courier left our headquarters laden with presents for our friends in England. I soon received a complaint from the Captain of one of the gunboats operating this run, saying that he could not tolerate the stench of the somewhat high Camembert cheeses which we were sending over. Charlie Head and I decided to change to millinery, a more easily handled commodity. We made good friends with a milliner in Bayeux, who was also the local midwife. Several garments were dispatched to our wives. By chance the midwife-milliner had a figure very similar to that of Mrs. Head. Charlie's French had not improved a lot since the Algerian days and one day I heard the lady, after Charlie had ordered a brassiere for his wife, saying, repeatedly:

"Quel numero?"

Charlie merely pointed to the lady and said several times: "Comme ci, comme ça."

This time the French did work. After this we thought we must ask the lady to come over and have tea with us. She hitch-hiked to our headquarters, but on asking the very efficient sentries at General Dempsey's headquarters for "Charlie 'Ead, beret vert," was unfortunately turned away.

At last, in mid-July, came the break-out. The prelude was a Bomber Command offensive immediately in front of the Commando positions. Four thousand planes, mostly heavy bombers, blasted the German positions. The enemy replied in a small way over Le Plein. Ironically, of the two bombs dropped, one landed in the cookhouse of 4 Troop and the other set on fire three lorries loaded with ammunition on the edge of 5 Troop area. A sergeant, who was upstairs in the cookhouse when the bomb burst, flung himself on to his bedspace only to find that the blast of the bomb a split second before had blown that particular section of the floor away. When he landed on his head in a pile of bully beef tins twelve feet below, his language was a little lurid.

Information along the whole front indicated that the enemy had started to withdraw and the prearranged pursuit was put into operation. The 1st Commando Brigade advanced through Le Bois de Bavent, with No. 4 Commando leading to clear and mark the route through the woods for the remainder of the units to follow. They reached the area of Bavent without contacting the enemy and without casualties from mines or booby traps. The enemy was obviously conducting a carefully planned withdrawal and had been able to evacuate all their equipment and weapons. No. 3 Commando moved on towards Varaville where they made contact with the enemy rearguard, caught in the village by the speed of our follow-up, but the village was cleared without much trouble. No. 6 Commando was in Bavent and 4 Commando to the south, with 45 Royal Marine Commando in reserve. On the 19th August the brigade was ordered to attack and hold a section of the high ground north of the main Dozule road, to cover a further advance on to Dozule and to exploit to the east as soon as circumstances permitted. The height was to be in our hands by dawn. This operation was a race against time—Derek Mills Roberts, the Brigade Commander, had to formulate his plan on the way back to his headquarters. He decided that an approach by stealth was the only way, avoiding all obvious routes. All available bridges over the canal east of the Dives had been blown, and an infantry bridge had to be constructed by 6 Airborne Division Royal Engineers.

No. 4 Commando, whose objective was L'Epine, crossed the start line first and advanced along the line of the railway. The main body of the brigade crossed twenty minutes later, moving in single file with 3 Commando leading, followed by 45 Commando and 6 Commando. A difficult route was deliberately chosen in order to increase the chance of surprise, and the night was exceptionally dark. Close formation was maintained, but each time the way was reconnoitred the whole column had to halt and get down, and progress was slow. At 6.15 a.m. the leading section struck the enemy Company Headquarters. Surprise was complete, and the first indication that the enemy had of the attack was when their sentries were shot and the headquarters surrounded while they were at breakfast. The whole brigade had managed to infiltrate right through the enemy forward defence lines, and it was later learnt that our troops had passed undetected over a bridge which was covered by a machine-gun position manned by seven Germans, less than 150 yards away. Brigade Headquarters settled in the area of the captured enemy headquarters with 3 and 6 Commandos in protection of the proposed supply routes.

In five days the brigade covered forty miles, advancing mostly by night and on foot and fighting strenuous actions on the way. By the 26th August, however, the enemy had gone over the Risle and the Seine and the order was to dispose the troops with a view to maximum rest and comfort without tactical considerations. The brigade had been in the fight for eighty-three days without being rested. Of the 146 officers and 2,252 other ranks who had landed on D-Day, seventy-seven officers and 890 other ranks had become casualties. One of the casualties in the final advance of No. 3 Commando was Michael Woydevodsky, who was hit in the neck by a bullet fired from a machine gun on the far bank of the Seine. The bullet remains in his neck to this day. He was evacuated to England where Allied Control seized on him as a speaker of Russian and, much against his will, he was employed interrogating Russians for the rest of the war. The 1st Commando Brigade was then recalled to England to reorganise and prepare for the war in the Far East. They were due to leave in the autumn. Peter Young was promoted full to Colonel and left to take over second-in-command of the 3rd Commando Brigade, then operating in Burma. Arthur Komrower took over No. 3 Commando. I felt very proud of them and wondered when I should see them again.

My headquarters had followed close on the heels of this advance. It was fun to get moving again.

By this time Charlie Head's leg had become so bad that it was obvious he would have to leave us for treatment. He had dinner with General Dempsey on his last night. Everybody was very depressed at losing him. We all tried to drown our sorrows in alcohol but without success. Next morning everyone, from officers to privates, felt close to tears as Charlie limped off to his jeep.

"I don't know what I'm going to do, John," he kept saying. "Don't send me home!"

But Charlie by now could scarcely walk. His leg had swollen terribly. I was afraid he would die without proper medical attention. I sent for Allan Peile to take his place.

No. 4 Commando Brigade had been advancing at an equally fast rate near the coast. They carried right on over the Seine, and took a big part in the capture of Le Havre. In Le Havre they came across the German equivalent of the N.A.A.F.I., heavily stocked with food and wine! I sent Allan Peile with a jeep and trailer, and he brought it back piled high with brandy and champagne. As an afterthought, Allan put in a keg of Danish butter weighing 200 lbs.

After the fall of Le Havre No. 4 Commando Brigade were given a well-earned rest. My headquarters was temporarily out of commission and I looked round for somewhere more comfortable for them to live. I had always told my officers to look after their men as well as was humanly possible, sometimes using the phrase, "If you can put them in the Ritz Hotel, do so. It won't be too good for them." Accordingly, when Paris fell, we moved to the Ritz in Paris. The management was co-operative, charging officers one pound a day and other ranks ten shillings. The ten shillings did not come from the the soldiers' pockets. The officers clubbed together and pooled all their francs. It was a first-class headquarters, as everybody knew where to find us. A good time was had by all.

All sorts of interesting characters were to be met in the Ritz Hotel: some were genuine and some were not. The rich French collaborateurs were most effusive but spoilt the favourable impression they were trying to create by ending their welcome with the words, "Pour nous la guerre est finis." Among the best and most genuine types I met at the Ritz were the late Christopher Buckley, ace war correspondent of the *Daily Telegraph*, Douglas Williams, who still works for the same newspaper, and Bill Paley, head of Columbia Broadcasting System.

After a few days we ran out of money and I suddenly thought of the keg of butter. It was a question of leaving Paris or doing something about our financial situation, so I told Allan Peile to take the butter and sell it in a black market restaurant. Good butter was unobtainable in Paris at that time. Allan came back in about twenty minutes with a wad of notes to the value of a hundred pounds sterling. This enabled us to carry on for a few days.

While in Paris, I drove Cathleen Mann to General Omar Bradley's headquarters near Chartres. Cathleen had an appointment to paint the General, and, having a day off, I decided to take the opportunity of visiting this important American headquarters. The Americans were charming to us when we arrived and General Bradley told me I was at liberty to look round as I pleased. This was exactly what I wished to do. I found the set-up was very similar to that of Monty's or Dempsey's Tac. H.Q. The caravans were a little larger and better, but the same calm and efficient atmosphere prevailed. As the end of the sitting drew near several of General Bradley's young staff officers appeared to admire the almost completed painting. They stayed rather a long time and the General remarked:

"Are you admiring the picture or the artist?"

They were equally good to look at.

When the painting was finished I was able to have a talk with the General who forecast with great accuracy the forth-coming trend of events. He was mad keen to get supplies forward to General Patton, and thought the war could be finished quickly if Patton were given full support. He foresaw exactly the fact that the Germans would settle down and fight bitterly if they were given a breathing space. I know nothing of the intimate details of the alleged rivalry between Generals Bradley and Montgomery at a later stage, but I do know that at this stage they liked and respected each other. My personal opinion is that the war could have been won in the autumn of 1944 by giving full support either to General Montgomery or to General Bradley and not by dividing the support between each of them. After a couple of most enjoyable drinks with the Americans I drove the artist back to Commando Group Headquarters at the Ritz.

All good things come to an end, however, and we left Paris for north-east France late in August, as things were on the move again. We set up Tac. H.Q. at the Chateau Coucou, near Cassel. No. 4 Commando Brigade were near us, helping to contain and harass the Germans who were still holding out at Dunkirk.

Chapter XIV

AND SO TO GERMANY

IN MID-SEPTEMBER, 1944, General Sturges ordered me to
return to England. There was not sufficient work for me to
do in looking after the interests of No. 4 Commando Brigade
only. I left Allan Peile with a skeleton headquarters to help in
any way that might be necessary. No. 4 Army Commando was
transferred to No. 4 Commando Brigade at this time, in order
to have an army Commando working with the Royal Marine
units of that brigade. Simultaneously, No. 46 Royal Marine
Commando was transferred from 4 Commando Brigade to 1
Commando Brigade.

The resources of the Royal Marines in the matter of providing
suitable officers had been heavily drawn on, owing to casualties,
and we managed to persuade the Royal Marine Office to allow
a number of army officers to be posted to Royal Marine
Commandos. This was a happy arrangement. The army
officers enjoyed serving with the Royal Marines, and the
marines benefited from the influx of new ideas and the contented volunteer atmosphere which the army officers brought
with them.

There was plenty to do in England. I was able to help No. 1
Commando Brigade in the work of reorganising for the Far
East. I also went round our training establishments seeing that
the new lessons from the European operations had been passed
on. We also had to send many reinforcements to No. 2 Commando Brigade in Italy and to No. 3 Commando Brigade in the
Far East. The men now coming into the Commandos were
young, but had a good spirit and were eager to learn. They
soon assimilated the Commando traditions.

I was also able to take a little leave. It was good to get
round London again.

One day when I was with some friends in London the King
of Greece rang up and said he would like to come to dinner with

them. It was a Sunday evening and no servants were available and last-minute telephone calls to the catering departments of our larger hotels proved abortive, so we got to work with the limited supply of food at our disposal. I knew the King quite well as I had met him in India before the war and again in Gibraltar. My particular role was to prepare a dish called Pomme Anna, made up as follows:

> 3 or 4 large potatoes
> 1 thinly sliced onion
> ¾ lb. grated cheese
> Pepper, salt, meat extract
> ½ pint water

Peel and slice potatoes; dissolve ½ teaspoon of meat extract in the water; line a pie-dish with alternate slices of potatoes, onion and grated cheese, with a final layer of potatoes on top. Season each layer, pour over the water. Bake for an hour. ——

Wasn't this a dainty dish to set before a king? The King was extremely pleased and ate a large portion, which was a compliment as he was rather delicate and had to be careful about his diet.

At the end of September, 1944, the first plans were formulated for an attack on the island fortress of Walcheren, to be made by Brigadier Leicester and 4 Commando Brigade in conjunction with the Canadian Army. The rapid advance of the British and American armies through France and Belgium had made the need of a large-sized port imperative in order to maintain these forces on their drive to the east. Antwerp had magnificent port facilities but these were of no use until the approaches to Antwerp, the territories bordering the Scheldt, had been cleared of the enemy, so with this object in view an assault on Walcheren was to be carried out in order to free the Scheldt from domination by German guns. Before this assault was to be made the south bank of the Scheldt had to be cleared and south Beveland sealed off.

The 2nd Canadian Corps, commanded by General Simonds, was in charge of the operation. Early in October a letter arrived from General Simonds to say that he was not happy about things, as far as the Commando planning was concerned. General Sturges told me to fly at once to Brussels to see what was wrong.

I went to see General Simonds. We had many friends among the Canadians from the Dieppe days so I felt at home in his headquarters. General Simonds said:

"This Walcheren planning isn't going at all well. Leicester keeps stressing the difficulties. I'm not happy about things."

I told him I thought he had misunderstood Leicester's mentality and that maybe Leicester was quite right to stress the difficulties. General Simonds was not convinced.

"I don't like it," he said.

"Leicester's the type of man who approaches the operation carefully," I said, "and then fights like a lion in the battle."

The General lent me his Buick. I drove straight down to see Jumbo Leicester, who had No. 4 Commando Brigade concentrated for training and briefing on the Belgian coast near Ostend. I went carefully through the planning with him, and found that there were indeed many difficulties. General Simonds came down the next day and everything was smoothed out. I said to him:

"You wait and see. Leicester will do a great job."

It is so much better to have a man like Leicester who approaches an operation carefully and then carries it out brilliantly, than to have the talkative type who is full of confidence before the operation and then fails in the battle.

The Island of Walcheren is composed of a rim of high, soft sand-dunes, varying from forty to 130 feet in height, in the centre of which is a low-lying, flat plane. It was decided to flood this plane so as to confine the Germans to the sand-dunes. On the night of the 3rd October a force of Lancasters breached the dyke at Westkappelle, the inhabitants having previously been warned in a broadcast by General Eisenhower. The Germans were thus confined to the sand-dunes. It was then planned that 4 Commando Brigade should assault the island through the breach in the dyke, taking the defences from the rear, exploiting along the sand-dunes in amphibians. It was a dirty, slogging operation, involving continual attacks on pill-boxes, but I felt that Leicester and his brigade would carry it out. The army Commando in the brigade, No. 4 Commando, was to assault the town of Flushing. By this time the Canadians had cleared all the land on the west bank of the Scheldt, after bitter, uncomfortable fighting in wet and cold weather. They had also forced their way up the narrow neck of land which joins Walcheren to the mainland of Holland. All was now set for the seaborne attack.

At that time of the year, November, conditions were not expected to be good, as rough seas and high winds, or fog were likely to prevail. In addition, the German defences were formidable. At least eighteen batteries covered the sea approaches; there were six anti-aircraft batteries, and mine-fields were extensive. It was also known that a rocket-projecting battery was positioned in the sand-dunes at the northern tip of the island, and another south-east of Westkappelle. Prisoner-of-war interrogation informed us that radio-controlled demo-lition vehicles, known as Goliaths, were kept behind the dunes between Domburg and Vrounenpolder.

I attended a good many meetings with the naval Commander, Admiral Sir Bertram Ramsay, but Jumbo Leicester was well able to handle his own affairs and I did not need to do much talking. I foresaw bitter fighting but was entirely confident of the result, and told General Simonds that, given a fair landing, 4 Commando Brigade were sure to capture the island of Walcheren.

The assault was planned in two phases: 4 Commando were to land at Flushing at first light, cross the Flushing Gap and link up with 4 Commando Brigade, consisting of 41, 47 and 48 Royal Marine Commandos, who were to land in the area of the Westkappelle Gap and clear the dunes of defences.

The weather prevented the proposed bomber attack on the coastal defences, with the result that about ninety-five per cent of the enemy guns were fully operative when the force approached Westkappelle in broad daylight. The naval support squadron therefore had to offer themselves as a target to the coastal defence guns in order to distract their attention from the landing force while it beached. No. 41 Royal Marine

Commando took the Westkappelle village and area, including the battery, and 48 Commando took a radar station and a stretch of dunes to the south-east. As night fell 41 had reached Domburg, fighting by the light of blazing houses.

The next day the weather prevented tank-landing craft from beaching: casualties could not be evacuated nor food and reserves brought ashore. The German opposition was very keen and machine-gun fire so intense that the members of one troop were all killed or wounded as they went into attack. No. 4 Commando had encountered severe machine-gun and cannon fire as they landed at Flushing but Jumbo Leicester's planning was so thorough that each man had studied air photographs and maps and had an exact knowledge of his individual task before he went into action. By night-fall 4 Commando had taken Flushing, and the north shores of the Scheldt were virtually free of hostile forces. No. 4 Commando then linked up with 47 Royal Marine Commando and reverted to the command of 4 Commando Brigade in order to subdue the enemy at the extreme north of the island. Casualties had been heavy: one amphibious vehicle with thirty Commandos on board hit a mine and no one survived.

By the 8th November, field guns reached the island from south Beveland and heavy concentrations were brought down on the last centres of resistance. At 6 a.m., 4 Commando requested that all air and artillery support be stopped since the Germans were ready to discuss surrender terms and Walcheren was entirely in our hands. Over two thousand prisoners had been taken and 4 Commando Brigade had given another first-rate performance.

General Simonds and the Canadians were delighted.

"You were quite right," he said.

"Yes," I said, "I hope it will be recognised."

It was. Jumbo Leicester received a Bar to his D.S.O.

Allan Peile was still running a small Commando Group Headquarters nearby. I moved in with him and we continually visited No. 4 Commando Brigade, which had now moved to Beveland Island, a position from which they dominated the surrounding countryside in their traditional manner. A flotilla of landing craft was attached to them and Jumbo Leicester launched nightly small-scale raids to keep the neighbouring Germans in the correct state of apprehension. The brigade's line covered the islands of Walcheren and north and south Beveland. Between the end of November, 1944, and the end of the war, this brigade made twenty active patrols, fourteen reconnaissances and half-a-dozen three-day patrols, in these very difficult surroundings.

Admiral Sir Walter Cowan came out to stay with us. Admiral Cowan was over seventy and had retired from the navy before the war. He longed to see further action and I think his ambition was to die on the battlefield. After fighting with the Eighth Army in the desert he joined the Commandos in Italy and won a bar to his D.S.O. at the age of seventy. Now he was on the spot again, longing for action. He loved the Commando atmosphere. I took him with me every day on my visits, but he was not satisfied. Things at this time were too quiet for him.

I was happy on the Continent and didn't want to go back to England. I liked the atmosphere and was on my own with no one to worry me. However, there was work to be done in England, and General Sturges recalled me again.

I started the old round, training establishments and general administration. There was also time for a little leave. One night I was with some very charming people playing one of my early games of poker. I found this a most intriguing game, especially in the company in which I was playing. Sitting next to me was Lady Stanley of Alderley, later Mrs. Clark Gable, and my concentration was rather affected. It was proving an expensive evening so when I finally held four two's I tried to get myself out of trouble. Lord Stanley on the other side of the table beat me with four three's. I hadn't time to worry about this, as the telephone rang, and I was told to go straight back to Belgium. No. 1 Commando Brigade, on the point of leaving for the Far East, had been recalled to north-west Europe as the result of the Battle of the Bulge.

I resumed my duties, running a small headquarters, linking up with General Dempsey's 2nd Army Headquarters at Achel in Belgium. Instead of the sunshine of Burma, No. 3 Commando were in snow-filled trenches on the line of the River

Maas, together with the rest of the 1st Commando Brigade. It was good to have them back.

The enemy by this time was retiring rapidly on Montfort, and Nos. 3, 6 and 45 Commandos began an assault on Maas-bracht, Brachterbeck and Montfortbeck. There was some hard fighting before the enemy was subdued, but the position was captured and held against determined counter-attacks.

One of the last objectives for No. 3 Commando in this area was the town of Linne on the east bank of the Maas. No. 4 Troop patrolled the town on the morning of the 24th January. A base was established in the churchyard and houses were searched. A Commando sergeant came face to face with a German whom he took prisoner, but the German refused to give any information, repeating over and over that he wished to die for the Fuehrer. However, it soon became apparent that the place was strongly held and the Commando withdrew to prepare for an attack supported by tanks.

Early next morning after a heavy barrage, No. 3 Commando assaulted Linne. It was bitterly cold in the town, thick snow covered the ground and it was difficult to dig in as the ground was frozen. The Germans were four hundred yards to the north, manning earthwork defences as there they had no houses. There were a surprising number of civilians in Linne, living for the most part in the cellars, often huddled under ragged blankets in squalor and confusion. I arrived to find No. 3 Commando having a very tough battle in the snow. Every movement in the street resulted in accurate shell fire from the Germans. At this inopportune moment some mail arrived and the post corporal started to deliver it. We advised him to wait a while but he took no notice and was shortly afterwards killed by a shell. The Commando was in wonderful form, but many familiar faces had now disappeared, as only the men with considerable time to serve were to have been taken to the Far East. A new set of characters had arisen and welded in perfectly with the remnants of the old Commando.

During a period when their troop was in reserve, I saw Roy Westley and another officer in a café having a great party with two German girls whose names were Helene and Marlene. This reminded me exactly of the parties Charlie Head and I had enjoyed in earlier days. The order which had gone out that there was to be no fraternising was obviously one to be ignored.

The next day Lance-corporal Selby and Trooper Connelly, driving in a jeep, mistook a turning in Linne and drove straight through the town into the German wire. A mine exploded and Selby was flung into the air with a fractured leg and severe shoulder injuries. Connelly was able to make his way back to our lines. With the explosion the Germans became alert, and flares and machine-gun fire made it impossible to rescue Selby. Two and a half days later a sentry reported a figure crawling in the road half-way between the two front lines. A jeep raced out and picked up a bloodstained Selby, who had spent nearly sixty hours without food or water and had improvised a tourniquet round his leg with his lanyard. Before being evacuated, Selby was able to give clear and accurate details of the German defences he had observed during his period between the lines.

Every man had a tremendous pride in his unit. It is very hard to say when No. 3 Commando was at its best. My own opinion would be before Dieppe or before Sicily. Nevertheless, it was plenty good enough at this time.

On the 12th February, 1945, No. 3 Commando was relieved by No. 46 Royal Marine Commando and went for a well-deserved rest at Maasbrecht. Brigadier Derek Mills Roberts still held command of the Brigade. He was an invigorating companion and used to like to walk me round in the snow in full view of the Germans, indicating to me the accomplishments of the previous night.

One night No. 46 Commando killed an entire section of Germans. When I saw them in the morning they were lying in the snow in perfect formation. An enormous German lance-corporal in the centre of the section had been carrying a Panzer-faust anti-tank weapon, somewhat like our bazooka. Derek turned him over with his foot.

"He's no nancy boy," he said, with a certain amount of pride.

General Dempsey was in great spirits as things were on the move again and the end was in sight. Sometimes I drove to the Dutch coast to get oysters, which were available at the rate of one cigarette for one oyster. The General enjoyed oysters and these still further improved our dinners. Allan Peile also developed a contact with a champagne firm at Rheims. He made a monthly trip, each time bringing back a case of forty-eight bottles at the rate of ten shillings per bottle. Most of this champagne found its way to the Commandos in the line.

Late in February there was a reorganisation along the whole front. The brigade was relieved by an American force. The final sweep of the Allied Armies up to the line of the Rhine took place in February and early March; 6 and 45 Commandos crossed the Maas to take part in the last attack, and No. 3 Commando relieved the marines at Smakt. The brigade was concentrated on the west bank of the Meuse and it was here that the final planning and training for the battle of the Rhine began. The Rhine is a great natural barrier to the very heart of Germany and the assault was planned as an amphibious operation. All manner of craft from canoes to Buffaloes were used in the specialised training to make the Commando river-conscious.

From the beginning we based all planning on a very heavy bombing raid to be made on Wesel on the night of the assault, and, in order to gain full effect, the assault troops had to enter the city almost on the heels of the R.A.F. The whole operation was called "Plunder" and the 1st Commando Brigade came directly under command of 12 Corps, who were to assault simultaneously with the 9th U.S. Army on the right and the 30th British Corps on the left. The crossing was to be made at night, and the following morning the 6th British Airborne Division and 17th U.S. Airborne Division were to drop east of the bridgehead and link up. The particular task given to 1st Commando Brigade was of vital importance; for on it depended the success of the whole crossing. This was the capture of the town of Wesel, the most important communication centre of the 2nd Army front, and the point at which the British and American forces joined. The brigade's plan fell into four sections. No. 46 Commando were to cross with Brigade Tac. H.Q. and secure a bridgehead in the area of Grav Insel. No. 6

Commando were to follow in storm boats and lead the way into Wesel, laying a white tape for the rest of the Commandos to follow, so that they could not lose their way. No. 3 Commando were to support in the amphibious Buffalo vehicles and help to consolidate within the town. Subsequently they were to clear the town and link up with the 9th U.S. Army to the south, and 17th U.S. Airborne Division to the east.

In the afternoon of the 23rd March, 1945, about six hours before the crossing was due to take place, Captain J. Alderson, former Commander of 6 Troop, No. 3 Commando, rejoined the unit, and, although still limping from wounds received in Normandy, took part in the operation. At 5.15 the code words went through denoting that the operation would take place that evening as planned, and within half-an-hour the first bombs from the Lancasters went crashing down into Wesel. In fifteen minutes over a hundred bombers had released their loads and departed. It was indeed a splendid prelude.

At ten o'clock in the evening the first Buffaloes carrying the Commandos lumbered over the bank and into the water. Shells continued to rain down but 3 Commando was soon ashore and ready to advance along the white tape already laid by No. 6 Commando. A second bombing attack took place on Wesel as 3 Commando were organising on the far bank. This support from bombers was highly appreciated. In the early days there had been no support at all and we had to look after ourselves.

No. 6 Commando cleared the way into the town, while 45 Royal Marine Commando and 3 Commando followed up and began attacking the defences and barricades. Counter-attacks were beaten off by 45 Royal Marine Commando, reinforced by 4 Troop of 3 Commando, which was established in a factory and an adjoining house on the north-east edge of the town. The Germans were confused by the sudden assault, and bombing, and their bewilderment increased on the morning of the 24th, when airborne troops poured from the sky and seized key positions in their rear.

By the afternoon of the 25th March, 3 Commando had cleared the centre of the town, which had been reduced to a mass of rubble, twisted girders and beams, smouldering fires, and precariously balanced walls verging on collapse. It was a scene of complete destruction. By the following morning the enemy had completely left the town, 850 prisoners had been taken together with important maps and documents. This completed one of the greatest operations of the war: skilfully planned, with tremendous air and ground support in conjunction with first-class troops, the battle had gone exactly to plan.

Meanwhile the might of the Allied armies was pouring over the Rhine and the armoured division raced across the Westphalian plain and into the Ruhr. On the 28th March, No. 3 Commando marched to Ruddenburg, where the Adjutant arranged an impromptu canteen at a farm, so that every man in the unit received two eggs and a glass of milk. The 1st Commando Brigade was continually on the move, never staying more than twenty-four hours in one place. The advance slowed down at Greven, and here we planned the attack on Osnabruck, designed to clear the routes through the city.

The plan was for the Brigade to capture a portion of the highest ground in the town and then spread out, each unit carrying out the various tasks allotted to it. In view of the heavy and accurate sniping, we decided that the break into the town should be made in darkness and the clearing of the routes begin at daylight. At 3 a.m. on the 4th April, 3 Commando led the attack on Osnabruck, by nine o'clock the brigade was firmly established, and by afternoon all the city west of the canal had been cleared. The bridges over the canal were finally cleared by 3 Commando. Thus the largest city yet occupied on German soil by British forces had been taken, with a total of 450 prisoners and fifty enemy casualties. The brigade suffered four killed and twenty-nine wounded. No. 3 Commando, greatly fatigued, were allowed a night's rest, much needed as they had been without sleep for three nights, and without a meal for twenty-four hours.

The following day they were again on the move and were placed under command of the 11th Armoured Division to force a crossing of the River Weser. Enemy opposition had stiffened considerably from the direction of Leese, and the plan was to cross the river and clear and occupy the village of Leese, which lay a mile from the east bank. The enemy had been reinforced with recruits from the 12th S.S. Training Battalion, and these had fanatical courage and first-class snipers.

The Commando crossed in assault boats and formed up under cover of the river bank, but anyone who raised his head above the level of the bank was shot, nearly always through the eye. The only solution was to break out at night and, after a long march round the right flank, to attack Leese from the rear. No. 6 Commando entered the town from the east, but the enemy had withdrawn. No. 3 Commando gave chase and caught the rearguard in the roads north of Leese.

Peter Bartholomew was in command and operated with tremendous skill and dash in these battles and river crossings. He had been with us in the early days but had returned to his regiment during the period of inactivity at Largs. He rejoined 3 Commando on its return to England in 1943. When the brigade returned to north-west Europe for the second time in early 1945, he was second-in-command to Arthur Komrower. With the lessons of John Pooley, Brian Butler and George Herbert in my mind, I decided that Arthur had done enough and posted him to the depot, leaving Peter Bartholomew to take over command.

On this patrol from Leese the leading troops suffered several casualties crossing open ground and Peter, seeing that his whole troop was exposed, immediately climbed on to a tank and, moving at speed up to the threatened point, personally directed the fire of the supporting tanks on to the centres of enemy opposition at close range. Standing on top of the tank, he was exposed to accurate machine-gun fire, and his runner, Corporal Joe Court, the man who started our friendship with the Canadians in the Dieppe days, was shot through the lung and knocked to the ground. He had to be evacuated but made a good recovery.

It was at this time that Captain John Alderson, who had rejoined 3 Commando before the Rhine crossing, was mortally wounded. He had consistently taken the lead, in the tradition of Algy Forrester. Ned Moore, still the medical officer, was evacuating the casualties from an open field and under heavy fire. Always, when one man fell there was another to go on. The impetus of the advance was always maintained in the Commando tradition.

On the 10th April the brigade proceeded to a small village near the River Aller, and planned another assault crossing. This was to follow the usual Commando method of night infiltration in single file, and it was hoped to rush a railway bridge lying half a mile north of a road bridge which the brigade was to secure. The railway bridge had been partly blown up by the enemy, but the leading troop of 3 Commando was able to scramble across and attack the enemy guard on the western bank. The brigade advanced to a knoll in heavily wooded country about half a mile east of the river, and here they encountered intense opposition from German marine troops who had been rushed from the north.

Just before 11.30 a.m. on the 11th April, No. 6 Commando launched an attack, and with bayonets fixed advanced through the trees at a fast double. Uttering terrible cries to curdle the blood of the German battalion, they raced through the wood, engaging the enemy who remained to fight and shooting down those who fled. By the end of the day, three hundred German dead were lying in the woods and nearly two hundred prisoners had been taken.

The brigade followed up the 11th Armoured Division towards the River Elbe, and was in Luneberg by the 19th April. This town was full of German hospitals and convalescent homes, and there appeared to be more German troops in the town than were British. They were, however, quite friendly.

Here we commenced the planning and training for operation "Enterprise," which was the name for the crossing of the River Elbe. This was very similar to the Rhine operation and was to start with intense artillery and air bombardment, followed by the usual night infiltration. The brigade's task was to cross the river on the right flank of the 15th Scottish Division, to capture Lauenberg and, if possible, the bridges over the Elbe-Trave Canal. The river was difficult to approach as the enemy side consisted of steep, thickly-wooded slopes, rising to between fifty and a hundred feet above the river at the point where we were due to cross.

The crossing took place on the 29th April under heavy fire from machine guns and twenty-millimetre flak guns. By 2 a.m., however, 6 Commando had established their bridge-head, and at three o'clock No. 3 Commando crossed in Buffaloes, moved to the back of Lauenberg and assaulted the town from the rear. No. 6 Commando captured intact the main bridge over the canal and, in spite of an increasingly active Luftwaffe, the brigade soon cleared the town.

Although the Russians were only fifty miles away, and there were few airfields left to the Germans, the Luftwaffe put on a great display. The sky was full of our 'planes and we had hundreds of anti-aircraft guns, but the Luftwaffe aces kept diving in, shooting and bombing, then pulling out of their dives to meet inevitable destruction from our guns and fighters. I lost another car from a direct hit in one of these raids.

Major Martin, still Administrative Officer of No. 3 Commando, was early across the river, and next day was in the leading elements of the 2nd Army to reach the Baltic. On the 11th November, 1918, this man, then Corporal Martin, 9th Lancers, was in charge of the leading patrol of the 2nd Army half-way across Belgium, when the First World War came to a conclusion.

The storming of the Elbe was No. 1 Commando Brigade's last battle; there was no more fight left in the Germans. Although the brigade took part in the pursuit to the Baltic, hardly a further shot was fired in anger.

A few days later, near Luneberg, where we had our head-quarters, I saw four German generals coming in to surrender to General Dempsey.

Dempsey had instructed his A.D.C. to place a small rug on the highly-polished floor at the bottom of four steps which the Germans would have to descend.

"I hope they slip up," General Dempsey remarked grimly. "I'd like to see them take a fall."

He didn't like the Germans much.

The enemy generals, moving with great care, disappointed Dempsey by retaining their dignity; but he was none too polite in his treatment of them. They left his room looking much less pompous than when they went in.

I now felt I could relax my concentration on the war. The race for the Two Thousand Guineas was approaching. Joe Lawson, the well-known trainer, had whispered to me, when I was in England early in March, that his horse, Court Martial, would win. Allan Peile wanted leave at this time. I told him he could have it on one condition, that he go to Rheims on his way, pick up forty-eight bottles of champagne and take them to England, paying the necessary customs duty. On arrival, he was to lodge them with William Hill as my stake on Court Martial.

Good champagne was hard to lay hands on in Britain at that time. Billy Hill valued the consignment at two hundred pounds, laying me a thousand pounds to the champagne. Thus, when Court Martial won, I had the thousand pounds awaiting me in England, plus my forty-eight bottles of champagne. This was a wonderful return for my money, for the champagne had cost me only twenty-four pounds. The customs man, in a victory mood, had not charged Allan Peile a penny duty. This meant I had won a thousand pounds for twenty-four, forty to one on a five to one shot. General Dempsey had other ideas about the race and thought that Dante was sure to win. I managed to persuade him to bet me twenty pounds to ten that Dante would beat Court Martial, so I also had twenty pounds to come from the Army Commander.

The following day I went to Lubeck and saw the 1st Commando Brigade comfortably established. It was the end of the war in Europe and my first love, No. 3 Commando, had come through it gloriously. The final campaign from the Rhine to the Baltic had been a fitting conclusion to everything. River crossings, night infiltrations, patrolling, fighting in the snow—all had been achieved with great success and no avoidable loss. I could not have envisaged a more glorious end to its operational life. Altogether eight D.S.O.s, more than thirty M.C.s, more than thirty M.M.s and five D.C.M.s were awarded to No. 3 Commando during its five years' existence. Everything asked of the unit had been carried out.

There was work to be done in England, so I said goodbye. Flying a brigadier's flag on the bonnet of a B.M.W. (which had been commandeered in the last days of the fighting to replace my loss from the bombing on the Elbe), I motored to Calais. I drove on to the boat, and a few hours later drove off again on to English soil, unopposed by the customs at Folkestone.

That's the way it went, and the way it would go if I had to do it again. For me, in many ways, it had been a wonderful war. Work hard, play hard, and take what is coming. Laughter and tears; hell and high water.